The
Transfigured
Cosmos

JON GREGERSON

THE
TRANSFIGURED
COSMOS

Four Essays
in
Eastern Orthodox
Christianity

Angelico Press

For information, address:
Angelico Press, Ltd.
169 Monitor St., Brooklyn, NY 11222
www.angelicopress.com

Paperback: 978-1-62138-658-2
Hardback: 978-1-62138-659-9

Cover design: Michael Schrauzer

THIS BOOK
IS DEDICATED
TO
CRIST LOUVDJIEFF

ACKNOWLEDGMENTS

For permission to use extracts from the following works, grateful acknowledgments and thanks are extended to:

A & C Black Ltd.: (Dacre Press): *Creative Suffering* by Iulia de Beausobre

Boston Book and Art Shop: *The Meaning of Icons* by Leonid Ouspensky and Vladimir Lossky

Dial Press: *Visions Rise and Change* by Pierre Van Paassen

The Eastern Churches Quarterly: *The Ascetic and Theological Teachings of (St.) Gregory Palamas* by Father Basil Krivosheine

Faber and Faber: *Early Fathers from the Philokalia; Writings from the Philokalia on the Prayer of the Heart; Unseen Warfare;* all translated by E. Kadloubovsky and G. E. H. Palmer

The Fellowship of St. Alban and St. Sergius: *On the Invocation of the Name of Jesus* by an anonymous monk

Harper & Brothers: *The Way of a Pilgrim* and *The Pilgrim Continues His Way*, trans. by R. M. French

Harvard University Press: *The Russian Religious Mind* by George Fedotov

Herder and Co.: *The Icon* by Alexei Hackel

S.P.C.K.: *The Church of the Eastern Christians* by Nicolas Zernov; *The Way of a Pilgrim* and *The Pilgrim Continues His Way*, translated by R. M. French

John M. Watkins: *On the Prayer of Jesus* by Bishop Ignati Brianchininov, trans. by Fr. Lazarus

FOREWORD

It is hoped that these essays will give the reader at least some small degree of insight into Eastern Orthodox Christianity, which on the whole remains little known in the West despite the fact that it is the religion of approximately 160 million people of the contemporary world. The first essay is a general introduction to Orthodoxy; the second is concerned with some of the basic elements of Russian spirituality; and the third and fourth deal with hesychasm—Orthodoxy's mystical tradition.

These essays are not to be understood as an exposition of Orthodox theology. The author is not a theologian, and the purpose of these essays is not to present Orthodox dogma and doctrine,* the verity of which the author takes for granted. Nor are they concerned with such matters as enumerating the Rules of St. Basil or giving a precise description of the "stages of contemplation." None of these fall within the scope of this book, which represents simply an attempt to convey something of the feeling and spirit of Orthodoxy, giving particular emphasis to Orthodox mysticism and stressing certain more or less unique aspects of Orthodox religious life and outlook.

Needless to say, many facets of Orthodox spirituality have not been dealt with in this book, and in it a number of generalizations have been made to which there are, quite naturally, exceptions. So, too, it should be noted that in many instances the Russian "form" of Orthodoxy has been stressed, since it is the one most familiar to the author.

J. G.

* For an excellent exposition of Orthodox doctrine and dogma the reader is referred to Vladimir Lossky, *The Mystical Theology of the Eastern Church*, London, 1957.

CONTENTS

ILLUSTRATIONS

Facing Page

EASTERN ORTHODOXY—AN INTRODUCTION

ORIGINALLY DEVELOPING in the Near East and Greece, Eastern Orthodox Christianity had by the end of the tenth century enveloped much of Eastern Europe, and it remains to the present day the chief spiritual tradition of the Greeks, Russians, Bulgarians, Roumanians, Serbians, and Georgians. Smaller communities of Eastern Orthodox faithful have also existed for many centuries in areas such as Syria, Egypt, Palestine, Albania, Finland, and Poland where other religions predominate. Greece and Russia have emerged through the centuries, however, as perhaps the most vital centers of Orthodox spirituality, the Russians also forming the largest branch of the Orthodox Church. Although each branch of the latter is headed by its own patriarch or archbishop, is autonomous, and preserves its own ethnic characteristics,* all are united by a common faith, doctrine, and ritual.

The religious experience of the Christian East is far from being identical with that of the West. Consequently, much in its "world outlook" is in many ways quite foreign to the Western Christian. Zernov summarizes some of the basic divergences of spirit that exist between Eastern and Western Christianity as follows:

> In the West body and spirit are clearly distinguished, and there is a tendency to set them in opposition to each other; in the Christian East they are treated as interdependent parts of the same creation . . . In the West

* For instance, each Orthodox church uses in its services both the language and music of its respective ethnic background.

the individual always occupies the center of attention; in
the East he is always seen as a member of a community . . . In the West mankind is the main object of
redemption; in the East the whole cosmos is brought
within its scope. . . . The West likes clear, precise
formulae; it is logical and analytic . . . The East treats
religion more as a life than a doctrine; it mistrusts overelaborate definitions . . . It believes that the Church and
its sacraments are divine mysteries . . . that they will always evade analysis by logical reasoning.[1]

The Western mind is analytic; it likes to scrutinize,
to dissect, to classify; in its dealings with religion it
tends to be logical and even legalistic. Eastern Christians, on the contrary are more interested in synthesis
. . . They look upon the world as one great organism;
they approach the diverse manifestations of life as an
expression of the same ultimate reality. . . .

The East does not think about salvation in terms of
the individual soul returning to its Maker; it is visual-
ized rather as a gradual process of transfiguration of the
whole cosmos, culminating in *theosis*† . . . Man is saved,
not from the world but with the world.[2]

Although Eastern Orthodoxy differs considerably from
Western Catholicism in points of emphasis, external form, and,
to a certain extent, interpretation, the two nevertheless are
based upon a common Sacred Tradition and thus have much
in common. Indeed, until 1054 the Orthodox Church was
united with that of the West, and the Christian Church
Eastern and Western was one. The separation which occurred
between them at this time was actually not so much in the
nature of a sudden severance as the culmination of many cen-

† Deification, a sharing through grace in the Divine life, partaking
of the Divine nature.

turies of gradual growing apart—and it may be viewed from several different perspectives. A dissimilarity of temperament, custom, and ethnic and historical background; a difference of understanding as to the hierarchal power and jurisdiction of the Patriarch of Rome; and various political upheavals of the time were all important factors involved in the separation of the two.**

While in spirit, the gulf between Western Catholicism and Eastern Orthodoxy has grown wider through the centuries, they nevertheless remain in agreement on the major portion of Christian doctrine, for they are both forms of "traditional Christianity." On the other hand, Eastern Orthodoxy has almost nothing in common with Protestantism, from which it is separated not only by the differing perspectives of East and West but also by the vast majority of its doctrines; its firmly rooted traditionalism and catholicity; its priesthood and concept of the Church; its sacramental life, icons, and elaborate liturgical ceremonial; its profound veneration of the Mother of God and the Saints; its contemplative monasticism and resplendent mystical tradition.‡

Eastern Orthodoxy is not based solely upon the historical Person of Christ but also upon Sacred Tradition as it has arisen under the guidance of the Holy Spirit within the common consciousness of the faithful, who, both living and dead, comprise the Mystical and Living Body of Christ. The total Sacred Tradition of the Church is a cohesive unity, and any sundering

** It should perhaps be mentioned here that at this time there had also arisen a rather subtle theological divergence between East and West as to whether the Holy Spirit proceeds from the Father or from the Father and the Son. The Orthodox Church maintains the former.

‡ It may be noted here that although there are some Orthodox delegates on the so called "World Council of Churches," they are present merely as witnesses of Orthodox Truth so that the Orthodox point of view may be presented. Orthodox collaboration with the Council is limited to secular and non-theological matters.

of its wholeness through fragmentation or individualistic interpretation is alien to the Orthodox spirit.* Doctrine, dogma,
and the mystical tradition, together with their "external" manifestation in sacraments and liturgical rites, in icons and even in
the church edifice itself, all form closely interrelated and inseparable "parts" of the total Sacred Tradition. Accepting through
Grace the entire sacred teaching of the Church as revealed by
God for the salvation and sanctification of man, each individual within the Mystical and Living Body of Christ perceives
the sacred truths according to his own capacity, experience and
level of understanding. But he always subordinates his own
individual limitations of understanding and experience to the
catholic, "supraindividual" experience of the whole Mystical
Body.

As celebrators of the sacred mysteries and bestowers of
sacramental Divine Grace, the priests and bishops of the Orthodox Church† are indispensable to the life of the Mystical Body.
They have basically the same priestly and episcopal functions
as the priests and bishops of the Catholic Church of the West,
and like the latter maintain unbroken the Apostolic Succession.
Nevertheless, several differences between Orthodox and Western Catholic clergy may be observed. Orthodox parish priests,
for instance, are generally married men, for Orthodoxy does
not require celibacy of her priesthood.** On the other hand,
Orthodox bishops, unlike those of the West, are in theory at

* Having arisen within the Sacred Tradition and forming a part of it,
Holy Scriptures, too, can be validly interpreted only within the *pleroma*
or fullness of the Church's consciousness. It may be noted that in Eastern
Orthodoxy, Bibliolatry and naively rationalistic Biblical criticisms are both
unknown.

† Unlike Western Catholicism, the Orthodox Church has also maintained a distinct order of deacons, who function as assistants to the priests
in the celebration of the sacred rites.

** Marriage, however, must occur before ordination. Hieromonks or
monastic priests are, of course, celibate.

least chosen only from among monastic priests.‡ Of considerably greater significance is the fact that the Patriarchs of the Orthodox Church neither individually nor collectively hold the same position as the Patriarch of Rome in the Western Church. "No one can pretend to personal infallibility in theological matters, and such infallibility attaches to no single office,"[3] writes Father Bulgakov. For the Orthodox, the Divinely given truths of the Sacred Tradition do not rest with the hierarchy alone and especially not with a single hierarchal office, but rather with the whole Church under the guidance of the Holy Spirit. The cohesion, unity, and strength of Orthodoxy lie neither in hierarchal authoritarianism nor in highly centralized institutionalism, but rather in the wholeness and certainty of the inner experience of the faithful.

Any rationalistic approach to the Divine mysteries, either in their broader meaning of all aspects of the Sacred Tradition or in their more specific meaning of the sacraments, is alien to the Orthodox spirit. In general, Orthodoxy is content to let mysteries be mysteries, not being given to such explicit, abstract exposition of sacred truths as is common in the West. Knowing, experiencing, and living the Divine mysteries, what need has Orthodoxy to formulate overelaborate definitions of them?

For many centuries, two aspects of Eastern Orthodoxy have taken precedence over all others—its devotional, sacramental, and liturgical element and its monastic, contemplative, mystical element. And it is into these two channels that most of the religious energy of the Orthodox world has been directed. Thus Orthodoxy has not laid nearly so much stress as the West on developing a "systematic" theology and philosophy. Further-

‡ In practice, this is not always the case. A non-monastic priest whose wife is dead or consents to become a nun, may also be elevated to the rank of bishop without ever having resided in a monastery, although he must take the monastic habit prior to the elevation.

more, knowing that material and social "progress" has no connection with the "realization of the Kingdom of God," and that the teachings set forth in the Sermon on the Mount can never be realized by society as a whole but only by the holy man, Orthodoxy has not fallen under the spell of an illusionary ethical idealism and sterile "humanitarianism." Its concern has rather been with worship and penitence, with prayer and contemplation of the "world invisible," with means and methods of salvation and awakening.

It is to monks, hermits, and other types of holy men that the Orthodox faithful look for both transforming, sanctifying influence and a deeper understanding of revealed sacred truths, as it is these holy men alone who look with clarity and purified vision upon the mysteries of God. Monasteries are "schools of awakening," and they occupy a place of paramount importance in religious life throughout the Orthodox world—from the deserts of the Near East to the frozen lakes of Finland and the dark forests of northern Russia. Regarded by many as the center of Orthodox contemplative life is the Holy Mountain of Athos in Greece where there are innumerable hermitages and more than twenty monasteries in which many thousands of monks and hermits seek liberation in God and preserve the Christ-given initiation.

The aim of Orthodoxy is the sanctification of man and cosmos, of the whole of life, through sacraments and sacred objects, through the blessing of the good things of this earth and through exorcisms. Experiencing the Divine as something essentially immediate, Orthodoxy is profoundly aware of the all-pervading Presence of God and has never ceased to celebrate the indwelling sanctity of the earth,* which it has always

---

* Orthodoxy is indeed also deeply aware of the presence of evil in the world, but it has never made the mistake of equating this evil with "materiality." So, too, it has always seen the "dominion of Satan" in the world as a secondary and counterfeit dominion subject to the Wisdom and Providence of God.

seen as overshadowed by and enclosed within the Light and Glory of the Saviour's Transfiguration. Such an awareness finds different forms of expression. It is manifest in the serene joyfulness of those Orthodox saints who heard the name of God in every sound and experienced His mysterious indwelling of every creature; it is manifest in the "externals" of Orthodox worship—in its rich ceremonial and elaborately decorated churches, dazzling with the brightness of every color in the spectrum. And it is here in its immediate and sensuous character that an essential aspect of Orthodox spirituality is to be found. "The Divinity is accessible through matter," writes Fedotov, "it can be not only seen, but even smelled, tasted, kissed."[4] Sacred sounds, actions, persons, and objects all function as channels of Divine Grace and vehicles of sanctification. Thus in the sacraments,† in holy men, in relics, and in icons the Divine Presence is immanent or localized in a very particular sense.

The importance of icons in Eastern Orthodox spirituality can scarcely be overemphasized. Indeed, they embody the innermost depths of Orthodox religious experience. An icon is a painting on wood of Christ, the Theotokos (the Mother of God), or a saint, representing their participation in the fullness of the Divine Life. While most icons portray but single Holy Ones or scenes from their lives corresponding to the feasts of the liturgical cycle, others give expression to various mystical intuitions such as the Hagia Sophia or Divine Wisdom. Many are partially covered with ornate gold or silver metalwork, which is sometimes inlaid with brilliantly hued enamels. They may be hung on walls, laid on small altar-like stands, or set permanently in elaborate shrines—and before every icon burns a hanging lamp celebrating the mysterious Divine Presence. In a traditionally Orthodox society, icons are

† Today the Orthodox Church reckons the mysteries or sacraments as seven in number. They are essentially the same as those of Western Catholicism.

found not only in churches and in the homes of the faithful, but also in shrines along the streets, in market places, public buildings, and taverns. In short, they are found everywhere, sanctifying all aspects of daily life and serving as constant reminders of the Mystery of the Incarnation and the sanctification of man and cosmos in and through God.

The Eastern Orthodox icon is not a mere symbol of the sacred figure or event represented as is the religious image in the West, for in and through it the respective sacred beings and events portrayed are made immediate. In a certain sense, they are present within the icon itself, which reflects the fullness of the Divine; no impenetrable gulf separates the Holy Ones from their images, heaven from earth, Creator from creature.

Many different materials go into the making of an icon, including wood, chalk, egg whites, water, and pigments of flowers, thus representing the mineral, animal, and vegetable kingdoms. So, too, sacred relics of the Holy Ones are not infrequently mixed with the paints. This participation of all creation in the icon serves to emphasize the indwelling sanctity of the entire created world and expresses its "sharing" in the Redemption.

Icons are never signed, and this outward anonymity corresponds with their inner message. Although they are made in strict accordance with the iconographic canon** from which

** In practice today this is not always the case. Unfortunately, under the impact of Western influence, the icons in many Orthodox churches in America very often manifest such an appalling neglect of the iconographic canon that they are hardly recognizable as Orthodox icons and certainly

The Mother of God ("Our Lady of Vladi-mir")—Russian icon

there should be no divergence, no two are exactly alike, except in cases when exact copies are made of particularly celebrated icons. Traditionally, Orthodox icons are made by contemplative monks; this, however, is not a necessity. Any pious layman of intuitive insight and talent, providing he follows the ascetic and sacramental disciplines proper to an iconographer, can make an icon.

Iconographers do not create sacred images as isolated individuals. Rather, they give form and color to the "supra-personal" intuitive wisdom of Sacred Tradition, a wisdom which is "personally" perceived only when one has been liberated from the enchantment of the fallen state. Ideally, the Orthodox iconographer should be a person who has realized the sanctified state. Then he is one with the sacred being whose image he creates.

The icon reveals not the ordinary fallen state with its attendant illusions, but rather the transfigured and Theocentric‡ state. It reveals the Divine world, the real world wherein time and space offer no limitations to the timeless, uncircumscribed reality of the Divine mysteries and the all-pervading Presence of God. Hence, in the icon no attempt is made to create the illusion of space or volume. Above all else the icon celebrates the mystery of transfiguration through holiness. In the words of Leonid Ouspensky:

> A man's transfiguration communicates itself to all the surroundings, for an attribute of holiness is the santification of all the surrounding world with which a saint

---

cannot be considered proper objects of veneration. Among other regrettable Westernizing tendencies in the Orthodox churches in America, most Russian churches being a noteworthy exception, may be mentioned the introduction of visible choirs and organs as well as of pews, all of which are quite alien to Orthodox Tradition and tend to destroy the true spirit of Orthodox worship.

‡ "God-centered."

comes into contact. Sanctity has not only a personal, but also a general human as well as a cosmic significance. . . . In accordance with this, all that is depicted in the icon reflects not the disorder of our sinful world, but divine order . . . a realm governed not by earthly logic, not by human morality, but by Divine Grace . . . This is why what we see in the icon is so unlike what we see in ordinary life. The Divine Light permeates all things, so there is no source of light which would illumine objects from one side or another; objects cast no shadows, for no shadows exist in the Kingdom of God.[5]

In the icon all is Theocentric; the cosmos itself is refulgent with the sanctity of the Holy Ones; the illusion, dispersion, and duality of the prince of darkness is banished; and the very mystery of Divinity is revealed in its infinite and eternal splendor.

Just as the icon has no third dimension in the ordinary sense, neither does it know "realism" in regard to physical characteristics. To Western eyes, the icon is indeed decidedly "unrealistic." In it the body becomes elongated and human features are freed of all coarseness, thus signifying a "refinement" of the senses and their full participation in the deified state. A profound sensitivity is expressed in the physical characteristics of the Holy Ones—in their long fingers, their small mouths, their finely-shaped noses, and the clear serene gaze of their eyes, all of which indicate their sanctity and the fullness and clarity of their perception of reality which is unblemished by sin, ignorance, or illusion. So, too, in iconographic scenes only those who have not realized the deified state appear in full profile, for "profile is already the beginning of absence."

To the Orthodox mind, images which are "naturalistic" cannot express the Presence of the Formless, Eternal, and Uncreated Divine Absolute. Thus the "religious" painting and sculpture* of the Renaissance and post-Renaissance West strikes most Orthodox as being purely secular in character. It is as if the created had usurped the throne of the Creator, as if the relative had replaced the Absolute. To make images of the Holy Ones as though they were simply ordinary human beings is to deprive them of all religious content and ignore their participation in the Divine Nature. Christ is man, but He is also God; the saints are men and yet through Divine Grace they have realized union with God and true participation in the Divine Nature. Similarly, to represent the cosmos in a sacred image as it appears in our ordinary consciousness and perception is to see it without God and minus His Presence.

The created and temporal finds its reality and wholeness only in and through the Uncreated and Eternal—and of this fact the icon is a constant reminder. Through the absence of "naturalism" or dimensional and anatomical "realism" in the icon, the "Divine dimension" is introduced and all things are revealed in the fullness of the Spirit of God.†

Attending the Divine Liturgy in an Orthodox church for the first time, a Westerner finds himself in completely unfamiliar surroundings. The entire atmosphere—the church edifice, the ceremonial, the music, the behavior of the worshippers and the appearance of the priests who traditionally have flowing beards and long hair—may indeed seem hardly less strange to him than that of a Far Eastern temple.

Every Orthodox church is an image of the macrocosm and also a center of the Divine Life. It is a place of epiphany where

* It may be noted here that although the Eastern Orthodox veneration of icons quite exceeds that given to any type of sacred image in the Western Church, statues are alien to Orthodox Tradition and hence none are found in Orthodox churches. This rejection of the sculptured image is closely related to Orthodoxy's objection to "naturalism" in iconography.

† Needless to say, non-traditional and non-iconographic modern "religious" art, however "non-representational" or lacking in "naturalism," is totally unsuitable for this purpose.

there is a particular localization of the Divine Presence, for within it the Divine mysteries are celebrated, and there are icons of great sanctity as well as relics of the Holy Ones who have realized deification in God. It is enveloped by a profound sense of mystery, and there is a feeling not only of God made manifest and immediate to the senses, but also of the hidden, intangible Divine Presence which eludes form, words, and sensuous perception. Throughout the church innumerable candles and hanging lamps burn before the icons, many of which are set in elaborate shrines. An odor of incense pervades the air, and in the east end of the church, hidden behind a towering screen set with icons and known as the *iconostas,* stands the altar upon which the life-bestowing Divine Sacrifice continues to take place in the now of eternity.

In most Orthodox churches a large dome, symbolizing the vault of heaven, rises above the nave and from it hangs an ornate *khoros* or chandelier which often holds several hundred candles. In monastic churches the various parts of the *khoros* are of a mobile nature. During "nights of watching" on great feasts, the huge chandelier is set slowly swinging back and forth in a rhythmic motion, the whole producing a strangely profound and joyous effect. Lit with a multitude of candles and set with glittering icons, each section of the chandelier moves within the whole, casting strange shadows on the walls and ceiling of the church and conveying a peculiar sense of mystery as the monks chant the Divine offices. To the monks the swinging chandelier represents the joyous dance of the angels and Holy Ones of all ages, rejoicing over the respective festival, celebrating a mystery within the Divine Life.

There is no pulpit in most Orthodox churches, and for the Orthodox, attending church does not mean going to hear a sermon but rather to participate in the Liturgy.** Nor do tradi-

** The Liturgy is usually but by no means always followed by a brief discourse generally on the significance of the particular feast day.

tionally constructed Orthodox churches have pews or seats, other than a few benches along the wall for the infirm. Thus a quality of unobstructed space not only gives to even the smallest churches a certain spaciousness, but also harmonizes with the sense of timelessness which pervades all Orthodox services. The feeling of confinement which is so characteristic of churches in the West is totally lacking and there is a freedom and spontaneity of action. One need not worry about being late to an Orthodox church, for the congregation is not expected to arrive at any specific time. The services, which are usually conducted in a leisurely, non-time-conscious manner, are long, lasting for at least two hours, and during them worshippers enter in a constant stream while others depart. Each person stands or kneels‡ wherever and whenever he is so moved and similarly is free to move around the church. Indeed, most Orthodox faithful upon entering the church "pilgrimage" from shrine to shrine as from mystery to mystery, lighting candles before the holy images, bowing, and prostrating themselves before them.

Compared with the ceremonial splendor and mystical profundity of the Eastern Orthodox Mass, the Roman Mass as celebrated in the average parish church of the West seems almost Protestant to the Orthodox. Not only is such ceremonial richness lacking in the West, but the whole feeling and spirit is quite different. "Compared with the Orthodox service," writes Fedotov, "the Roman liturgy makes the impression of greater distance between two worlds, one of ascetic longing, of thirst without quenching."[6]

As "low Masses" are unknown in the Orthodox Church, every Eucharist is celebrated in the fullness of liturgical tradition, the entire Liturgy—which is most frequently that of St. John Chrysostom and sometimes that of St. Basil—always being

‡ Kneeling for the Orthodox denotes penitence. Hence during the Easter services and for a number of weeks following no one kneels, as kneeling is considered inappropriate to the joyfulness of the Easter season.

sung or chanted by the priests, deacons, and choir. Amidst clouds of incense the officiants, dressed in elaborate vestments, celebrate the mysteries of the Divine Life, the Divine Word speaking with eloquent beauty in the drama of the sacred rites. Often the censers have tiny bells attached to them which make a tinkling sound every time they are swung. Everything in the church is censed many times—the sanctuary and altar, the icons, the Eucharistic elements, the celebrants, and the congregation; the flames of numberless candles dance and leap within the shadows, reflecting tiny jewels of light in the gold of the icons; blessings are invoked for the living and the dead, innumerable litanies are chanted, and prayers of penitence, thanksgiving, and praise are offered. The devotee enters the realm of the Eternal, worshipping God in His ineffable mystery and venerating the saints and the Mother of God while within himself he relives the events of the life of Christ—not as an individual isolated from God, but in the fullness of the Mystical and Living Body of Christ. The mysteries of the Divine Life are perceived in their timeless reality. The words of Christ at the Last Supper are repeated by the priest who—after having offered the holy gifts of bread and wine saying, "Thine own of Thine own we offer to Thee, in all and for all"—invokes the Holy Spirit to descend upon the bread and wine as well as upon the faithful. Gradually the Divine Presence is revealed in the metamorphosis or transfiguration of the bread and wine of the Eucharist into the Body and Blood of Christ. The Divine Sacrifice is made, the risen Christ is manifest, and streams of Divine Grace flood forth into the world. Heaven and earth, Infinite and finite, Uncreated and created, God and man come together and become one, or rather, their already existing unity is realized. "The Eucharist, for an Orthodox Christian," writes Zernov, "is not so much a sudden intervention from above, as a gradual revelation of the divine presence which is always here."[7] After the officiants, together with those members of the congregation who are properly prepared, receive the Holy

Eucharist,* the ancient liturgy proceeds, the service finally ending with the veneration of the Cross by all present.

The Resurrection is the greatest feast of the Church, and in traditional Orthodox iconography it is represented not as the rise of Christ from the tomb, but rather as His descent into Hell "when the gates of Hell were broken and the hinges shattered." As the Resurrection is the triumph of the Godman, it is also redemption of the past and liberation from Hell. The virtue and grace which issue forth from the Sacrifice of the Cross move backward as well as forward, for the events of the Divine Life are timeless and ever-present realities. Hackel, describing an icon of the Resurrection, writes:

> Christ has conquered Hell and He stands victorious on the broken gates of the palace of Hades. Under them in the Pit, lie demons deprived of their power. Christ helps Adam and Eve out of the tomb; thus sin is overcome. . . . In the background is the symbol of the cosmos—the triple circle. Its quiet light falls on the rocky landscape and on all creation. 'Everything is filled with a new light; Heaven and earth, and all that is under the earth.' And everywhere is heard the jubilant cry of Easter: 'Christ is risen, joy eternal.'[8]

Adam, Fallen Man, who in his state of illusion and inner dispersion is held captive by Hell, is liberated and sanctified in and by the Godman, Christ.

The joy and splendor of the Easter Liturgy almost defy description. At midnight, the bishop or the chief priest emerges from behind the *iconostas,* a lighted candle in his hand. The silence of the darkened church is broken and the Resurrection of the Christ proclaimed. "Come then and take light from the

---

* It may be noted that frequent Communion is not a common practice among the Orthodox laity, most of whom receive the Holy Eucharist only once or twice a year.

Light which is never extinguished," chants the priest. A tremendous clanging of bells commences and gradually the whole church becomes ablaze with light as the candles held by the faithful are lit, the flame passing from candle to candle. Then the clergy in golden vestments, carrying icons, banners, candles, flowers, and swinging censers, emerge from the church and together with the faithful form a procession which circumambulates the building. All return to the church where the sacred rites celebrating this great mystery within the Divine Life continue for many hours—and constantly is heard the joyous cry of the Resurrection: *"Khristos voskrese"* ("Christ is risen"), announces the priest in Russian churches; *"Voistinu voskrese"* (In Absolute Truth He is risen"),† respond the faithful.

The following description of the Easter Liturgy as celebrated at Yelocharsky Cathedral in contemporary Moscow marvelously conveys the spirit and feeling of the Orthodox Easter as well as Orthodox worship in general:

> Everything was turned into a vast, jubilating, triumphant joy; the golden priests and acolytes, the blazing altar, the rich icons, the ecstatic multitude, the walls, the pillars, the very roof, all creation, seemed to join as the choir sang: 'Stand in the Light; Oh, stand in the Light,

† The customary translation is given here. A more accurate translation and one which emphasizes the immediate quality of the Resurrection Mystery would be: "Christ is rising" and "In Absolute Truth He is rising."

His Holiness, the Patriarch of Moscow
blessing the faithful during church services
—Moscow, 1958
(Sovfoto)

ye New Jerusalem! For the glory of the Lord has come over thee. . . . O divine, O dearest, O sweetest voice of Thee who hast promised to remain with us unto the end of the age; O Christ, O Wisdom and Word of God. . . .'

It was as if they could not stop singing; as if time stood still, as if the tabernacle of God had descended amongst men. The multitude was stirred by something akin to the Prophet's divine intoxication. This was what made David dance before the Ark like a fool in God. The mountains clapped their hands for joy. The ocean leaped like a deer. The morning stars sang together. . . .

I saw why there is so little preaching and verbal exhortation in the Russian Church. The undercurrent of Orthodoxy's motive is to infuse something of holiness into everyday life. This is what the faithful carry away from the contemplation of the mystery.[9]

SOME ASPECTS OF THE RUSSIAN
RELIGIOUS CONSCIOUSNESS

ORTHODOXY IS one, and yet it is "many." One can speak of the general qualities and spirit of Orthodoxy as a whole, and one can also speak of the specific qualities and spirit of every ethnically different Orthodox people. Syrian spirituality is quite different from Roumanian spirituality, Greek spirituality is quite different from Russian spirituality. Each of these possesses certain more or less unique characteristics determined by its own ethnic, cultural, and linguistic background as well as by those certain qualities of spirit, mentality, temperament, and experience which every people possesses as more or less its own. Even in Western Catholicism, in which there is a much greater degree of uniformity, one can nevertheless observe something similar. The spirit of Spanish Catholicism is, for instance, very different from that of Irish Catholicism. In Orthodoxy, every different ethnic group has developed and enriched Orthodox spirituality in its own way. Doctrine and dogma are the same among all Orthodox peoples, but each people adapts itself to Orthodox spirituality according to its particular qualities of spirit and background.

This essay will deal with various aspects of the spirituality of one Orthodox people, namely the Russians; its concern will be with some of the basic elements of the Russian religious consciousness, some of which are also found in varying degrees among other Orthodox peoples, and others not. In doing this, it has seemed best to keep much of this essay within the context of traditional pre-revolutionary Russia.

Contrary to notions prevalent in the West, however, Russian Orthodox spirituality continues to flourish not only among Russian emigres in America, Western Europe, and elsewhere, but also in the Soviet Union itself. There are approximately one hundred monasteries functioning in Russia today and nearly as many convents; thousands of pilgrims still come to the holy places by foot; the Liturgy continues to be celebrated in thousands of churches; and at Easter untold millions receive Absolution and Communion. What was the Russian religious consciousness is still the Russian religious consciousness, and it is something deeply embedded in the Russian soul.

The Revolution caused considerable upheaval in Russian religious life, but by no means did it extinguish it. The persecution of the Church which lasted for many years has ceased, the state now contenting itself with atheist propaganda. The anti-religious policies of the Communist government, however, have not had a wholly negative effect on the Russian Church. Indeed, the latter has emerged considerably purified of the corruption which undeniably existed within it in the period immediately prior to the Revolution. Only those of genuine conviction and deep faith in the mysteries of the spirit remain within its fold. In short, Orthodoxy in Russia has suffered quantatively, but not qualitatively.

It is indeed probable that no other people within the Christian Tradition, either Eastern or Western, has been so absorbed by the spiritual quest as the Russians, whose thirst for the Absolute has amounted to hardly less than a passion. Nowhere outside of India were various types of holy men so

The Church of the Transfiguration—Kizhi,
Russia

common as in old Russia;* nowhere else was man so tortured by the desire to realize liberation and salvation in God. Such a "passion" for the Absolute was indeed more than mere wish for it on the part of the individuals concerned; it was an inner compulsion, an all-consuming flame grounded in the very depths of man's inner being, a flame which was quenched only when man had realized the wholeness and peace of the sanctified state. The Western notion of "poor clumsy Russia, so worried by the Holy Ghost," is indeed not inappropriate, for the Russians were "worried" by the Holy Ghost to an extent unknown elsewhere. Nobles would renounce their property and position, peasants their ordinary family and communal life, to become wandering pilgrims, "fools for Christ,"† hermits in the vast and silent forests of the north, or monks in one of the many monasteries that existed throughout Russia—from Archangel to Kiev and from Moscow to Irkutsk.

For the religious Russian, holy men are something real and not simply a vague ideal or abstraction. He has an unshakable belief that every particular *podvizhnik*** and sometimes, although more rarely, even an ordinary parish priest may truly be a *Bojy tcheloviek* or "man of :od" endowed through Divine Grace with special powers of sanctity, himself being an agent or vehicle of "extra-sacramental" Divine Grace and Wisdom. It was these holy men who formed the real aristocracy of old Russia and not the aristocracy of blood or social and economic prestige. The *podvizhniki* represented an "aristocracy of holiness," as it were, who came from all classes of

---

* It may be noted that until the eighteenth century Russian culture in all its aspects was either religious or folk. It was not until the reign of Peter "the Great" that Western secular culture began to penetrate Russia. This was the beginning of what many Russians have referred to as "the rotten wind from the West." Basically, however, Russian culture remained religiously oriented until the present century.

† See p. 39.

** An ascetic; one whose life involves "self-denial" and ascetic endeavor to the end of salvation and enlightenment.

traditional Russian society—from the highest nobility to the most lowly of peasants—for the path of the holy man or *podvizhnik* was open to all whose vocation was such, regardless of background. This "aristocracy of holiness" in a certain sense stood outside and above the conventional class structure of society, and before the most lowly and illiterate of simple peasant holy men the highest nobility and even the tsar himself might bow in humility and veneration, entreating a prayer or a blessing.

Basic to the Russian religious consciousness is its profound intuition of the Divine Kenosis‡—the spontaneous Self-outpouring, emptying and sacrifice of God which has its origin in His infinite Love. There are many different ways of looking at the Divine Kenosis, which understood in its widest possible sense takes several different forms and has a number of implications.

The Divine Kenosis is the very basis of the cosmos, which in its entirety proceeds from the depths of the Divine Life. Involving both the "outpouring of the Pre-existent One" in all created being, and the assumption by God of "the form of a servant" in and for His creatures, the Divine Kenosis is revealed in all the manifold aspects of God's relationship with His creatures—in His omnipresence and immanence in creation, His indwelling of even the most sinful of His creatures, His unveiling of Himself in the revelations of His Holy Spirit,* and above all else in the act of creation and the Incarnation.

The original act and continuing process of creation is kenotic in essence, for in it God "pours out" or "empties" Himself; in it "the Lamb was already slain" and continues to be slain. The Incarnation, too, is an outpouring or emptying of

‡ The adjectival form of kenosis is "kenotic." It should be observed here that actually there are no defined doctrines or dogmas of the faith concerning the Divine Kenosis as such. Thus this brief summary represents Russian religious thought rather than official dogma.

* E.g., in doctrines and dogmas regarding His Nature.

God, but in a very different sense from the act of creation. In the latter God remains hidden and unmanifest, but in the Incarnation—which represents the glorification and consecration of creation—the Word is made flesh, God becomes man and manifests Himself to man in the Person of the Godman.

Although in itself the Incarnation does not involve the "humiliation" of God any more than does the act of creation, the fact of man's fall together with the incarnate Word's subsequent offering of Himself on the Cross for all "from Adam to Antichrist" endows the Incarnation with an element of profound humiliation. Hence humiliation and lowliness are seen as important elements of the Divine Kenosis and are regarded as almost synonymous with it.

The entire life of Christ and all the qualities of His Person—His "taking the form of a servant," His lowliness, His baptism in the Jordan through which He acknowledged His taking the sins of the world upon Himself, the mockery he endured, and His non-resistant acceptance of the Cross—all reveal the Divine Kenosis. Nor did the Kenosis of Christ end with His crucifixion. The Resurrection followed the crucifixion, "the body of humility became the body of glory," yet the Divine outpouring and sacrifice continue even now, as is manifest sacramentally in the Holy Eucharist wherein the Body of Christ continues to be broken. It is the humiliated, Self-giving, non-resistant Christ, the incarnate God appearing among men as "the lowliest and least" "in the form of a servant" with no place to lay His head, Who forms the very core of the Russian religious consciousness. "There appeared among us One like unto us," writes Gogol. "Not in proud splendor and greatness; not as the chastiser of crime; not as a judge come to condemn."[1]

For many centuries before the Divine Kenosis as such appeared in Russian religious thought and theological writings, there was an almost unconscious application of its far-reaching implications in regard to the spiritual life. Man's salvation was seen as being intimately connected with the degree to which he imitated or one might say shared in and partook of the Divine Self-giving, sacrifice, lowliness, and humiliation. Such an attitude enters into nearly every facet of Russian spirituality; it may be seen in Russian asceticism and general world outlook; it may be seen in the lives of countless saints and ordinary laymen; and among the truly religious it led to a profound recognition of the presence of the indwelling Christ in the "lowliest and least,"† in beggars, in prisoners, and in the downtrodden—although, of course, in a very different sense than in the fully sanctified kenosis of the holy man.

The "kenotic life" not only involves lowliness and humiliation but also non-resistant acceptance of suffering, both spiritual and physical. This perception has found expression in Russian life in general and especially in the cult of "holy sufferers," a type of saint found only in Russia where they replaced, to a considerable degree, martyrs for the faith in the popular cultus. Boris and Gleb, the first Russians to be venerated as saints, were the first of a long line of "holy sufferers." In iconographic representations Boris is shown standing, a cross in one hand and in the other a sword, the end of which rests inactively on the earth to symbolize non-resistance. The innocent victims of a political plot instigated by their megalomaniac brother, Boris and Gleb submitted passively to a painful death at the hands of their brother's henchmen even though they had been warned of the plot and could have escaped its consequences through physical resistance if they had so desired. They were but ordinary laymen, albeit of princely rank, pious but not exceptionally ascetic, ready to submit to suffering and death but not with stoic detachment. Indeed, their "piteous helplessness" is a constant theme of the hagiography. The tears of Boris and the last words of Gleb—"Lo, I am being slain and I do not know what for"[2]—offer consider-

† It is interesting to observe that this notion during the last century gave rise to what was perhaps a somewhat exaggerated veneration of the "simple, lowly, God-fearing peasants" among the Slavophiles and others.

able contrast to the stern and impassive heroism which is generally thought of in connection with the Christian ideal of martyrdom.

Although kenotic suffering is, strictly speaking, innocent suffering, even that anguished spiritual suffering which is the result of sinfulness can be purifying and transfiguring; it too can be a self-emptying which flowers in experience of the infinite Divine Love and hence in love for our fellow creatures, in humility and in inward awakening. All suffering has the potentiality of being "creative" and sanctifying. Such an attitude toward pain and suffering has nothing in common with masochism; it does not involve any sort of morbid delight in suffering, but rather an acceptance of it as a basic reality of life. It involves perceiving that human life is not entirely separate from the Divine Life but in a certain sense exists within it. The suffering of man may be seen in terms of the suffering of Christ, Who sacrifices Himself even in the suffering of His creatures, giving Himself to them and preparing their spiritual transfiguration by means of it.

However much present-day Russians are subjected to the utopian idealism and secularism of the modern age, it is safe to assert that the basic Russian experience of suffering as a transfiguring and creative process will continue to exist. In the words of Sergei, Patriarch of Moscow (1943-44), "Where there is no suffering there can be no genuine following of Christ."[3]

Very revealing of the Russian religious consciousness is its veneration of "holy foolishness." Indeed, one of the most remarkable types of Russian holy man is the *Krista-rady yurodivy* or "fool for the sake of Christ." The holy fool is not easy to describe to the Westerner, not only because he is a more or less uniquely Russian figure but also because there are various kinds of holy fools. "God's fools" include those who become fools for the sake of Christ, acting the fool for the salvation of themselves and of others, "born fools" or simpletons of a saintly nature, and various types of saintly cripples, deaf-mutes, epileptics and the like.**

Ultimately, however, no precise lines can be drawn between these different types of holy fools, all of whom possess certain definite characteristics in common which immediately identify them as "fools in Christ." They all follow the kenotic way of life as manifest in their lack of earthly possessions and family, in their homelessness and in their certain indefinable sanctity; they all have keen spiritual insight and an immediate awareness of Divine mysteries; they all have a simple child-like wisdom and are given to actions which seem quite eccentric and not infrequently absurd to the eyes of the world.

Holy fools made a far greater appeal to the Russian religious consciousness than to the Byzantine, as is well illustrated in the fact that only one holy fool exists in the catalogue of Greek saints, while the Russians venerate as saints no less than seventeen.‡ St. Isaac of Kiev was the first Russian holy fool to receive the cultus of a saint. Playing games with children and foolish pranks on the abbot and brothers of the monastery where he lived, St. Isaac proved to be no small source of annoyance to these dignified Byzantinist monks, who nevertheless came to love his "foolishness in Christ" and began to take their own conventional dignity less seriously.

Throughout "Holy Russia" "fools in Christ" were to be found, some living on monastery grounds and others wandering from village to village, accepting whatever charity was

** By no means are all simpletons and the physically deformed regarded as holy fools, but only those who obviously possess a certain definite quality of sanctity and follow the kenotic way of life.

It should also be noted that the term "God's fools" includes all holy fools and is not limited to the relatively small number who were canonized saints.

‡ It is interesting to note that the famous St. Basil's Cathedral in Moscow derives its name not from St. Basil the Great, but rather St. Basil of Moscow, a holy fool.

offered them. So, too, nearly every village had its own holy fool. Sometimes he was to be seen playing with children, and sometimes sitting on a gravestone in the cemetery mumbling prayers or standing by the door of the church uttering enigmatic prophecies and chanting ancient ballads in such a jumbled manner that they were quite meaningless.

To the Russian mind, the holy fool is the "chosen of God" who, one might say, manifests the Divine Folly which is wiser than the wisdom of men. He is an innocent, an innocent who is, however, as "a dove with the wisdom of a serpent." He stands above "common sense," and to him the ordinary conventions of the world do not apply. There was for instance a holy fool who, except on fast days,* ate nothing but soft-boiled eggs, always wiping his hands, which were generally covered with egg yoke, on someone present, preferably someone spotlessly clean and well-dressed. Likewise, not a few holy fools have been known to meow like cats and make other strange noises during church services. Yet the actions of "God's fools" are not necessarily as "foolish" as they seem—and this is especially true of those who have become fools for the sake of Christ. Indeed, their "foolishness" and feigned madness is an ascetic endeavor, a means through which they share in the humiliation of Christ, a skillful means to induce humility in themselves as well as in others. They are, in a certain sense, masters of "sham," a "sham" which is inspired by God and therefore is not sham in the sense of deceit. This "inspired sham," however, does give them considerable insight into the inner state of ordinary men, giving them instantaneous knowledge as to whether or not a man's words and actions are sincere.

Having received through Divine Grace "the eye of wisdom" which many men spend their whole lives trying to acquire, the holy fool perceives things precisely as they are. Nor

* The Orthodox fast includes abstention not only from meat, but also from eggs and all dairy products.

is his vision limited to the inner state of men, for at all times he remains aware of the Theocentric quality of the cosmos.

> The *yurodivy* sees godliness and spirit shining out from all that is lowliest and 'worst'; from the dust of the highway, the sharp stones that cut his feet, the thorns that tear his flesh, the biting winter frost, the intolerable heat of summer, the stench of the doss house; from the most degraded types of men and women.[4]

Attached to nothing, settling nowhere yet at home everywhere, harassed by mocking children, a fool to the world, a jest to the "genteel," humble and accepting all things as the Will of God, he loves the entire cosmos. He loves the Divine Liturgy; he may understand very little of it intellectually if he is a born fool, yet he manifests part of the Reality it reveals. And he loves every creature and every grain of sand, although he generally minces no words when he encounters a deceitful or self-righteous man.

Holy fools have played no small part in Russian spiritual life, not infrequently acting as spiritual mentors, aiding men to awaken from illusion and attain salvation by means of some sudden action, an unexpected question, or a shower of abuse. An anecdote from the life of St. Tikhon Zadonsky affords a good illustration. Several versions of St. Tikhon's encounter with the holy fool exist, but the following one seems most complete. It is related that one day while St. Tikhon was sitting in the garden of the church pondering the mysteries of existence, a holy fool who had been wont to watch him from the cemetery adjacent to the garden suddenly ran up to him and slapped him on the face saying, "You thinkers are a lot of showy babblers. Don't think so highly of yourself." Tikhon immediately prostrated himself before "God's fool," who gave a loud laugh and ran back to the cemetery.

So too, the holy fools functioned as links between "the little father" (the tsar) and the people, mediators who kept the tsar in contact with the soul of the people, who always felt that as long as holy fools were revered by the tsars the realm would be assured of harmony and the benevolence of God. Indeed, the palace gates of the Kremlin remained open to the holy fools along with other types of holy men during the entire period of the Muscovite tsars,† most of whom, and especially Alexei Mikhailovitch "the Very Gentle and Most Pious," regarded them with great reverence. Often the tsars would spend several hours each day in their company, heeding their often rather obscure advice on matters of state and meekly submitting to their outspoken criticism and abuse in matters of personal conduct, criticism which would have entailed severe punishment if it had been made by anyone other than a holy fool. The latter could call the tsar "Herod" or "Judas"; he could severely rebuke the tsar for pride and self-righteousness; he could laugh at the tsar just when he was taking himself most seriously, and he could play absurd tricks on him; he could even strike the tsar or mimic him. Not only would the tsar endure all this patiently, but he would beg for the prayers of the holy fool, not infrequently only to receive a new shower of abuse if the latter thought the request came not from the heart.

Although the words and actions of the holy fool often seem "contrived" to bring about spiritual enlightenment and humility, this is by no means always the case. Sometimes there is an obvious purpose behind his actions, as in the case of the holy fool who slapped St. Tikhon, and sometimes there is no

---

† Beginning with Peter "the Great," however, the Westernized monarchy ceased to venerate the holy fools who indeed but seldom if ever gained access to the person of the tsar until the practice was revived by the last tsar, Nicholas II. He admitted all sorts of pilgrims and holy fools to the palace, seeking their advice, begging for their prayers, and enduring their insults in a desperate attempt to achieve harmony in his realm and regain the benevolence of God (especially in regard to his ailing son) and the people. But it was too late, and only too often the "pilgrims" and "holy fools" whom he and the tsarina venerated turned out to be satanic counterfeits of real holy men.

purpose at all. Not only is he a "spiritual mentor" and a manifestor of kenotic sanctity, but he is also a constant reminder of
the "Divine irrationality,"* to use Berdyaev's phrase. His
seemingly absurd words and actions coupled with his holiness
and spiritual insight quite clearly give to all an awareness of
the insolubility of Divine mysteries which cannot be grasped by
human reason. So too, in him and through him is manifest the
holy joyfulness of the pure of heart as well as what one might
call the "playful," spontaneous aspect of Divine Grace and
Wisdom and the "delight" of God in His creation.

. Quite in keeping with this one aspect of. "holy foolishness," folk tales‡ about "God's fools" reveal a delight in the
absurd and stress, although perhaps in a rather hyperbolic
manner, the holy fool's joyous and carefree abandonment to
the "Divine irrationality." Typical of folk tales dealing with
holy fools, the following delightful story is widely known
among the Russian peasantry.

One day Ivan the holy fool wandered into the forest
carrying a millstone which he had found along the road. Deep
in the forest, he climbed a tree and with much difficulty reached
the top with the millstone. He had not been there long when
a band of thieves, quite unaware of his presence, made camp
below and started to cook a large cauldron of soup. Feeling
rather playful, Ivan dropped the millstone into the soup, thereby
causing considerable havoc among the thieves, who ran off leaving behind them a cartload of stolen incense. Ivan came down
from the tree and, pulling the cartload of incense behind him,
wandered off to a cemetery where he put some of the incense
on top of a tomb and began to pound it with a mortar—a task

---

* Or, to use a more traditional term, one might say the "Divine
supra-rationality."

‡ It may be noted that here as well as in modern Russian literature
one not infrequently comes across the image of Russia herself as "a fool
in Christ." "Shall I not go on my knees before thee in the mire . . .
blessing the trace of thy bare foot, thou wretched, homeless, drunken
Russia—thou fool in Christ,"⁵ writes the poet Voloshin.

which occupied him for several hours. Suddenly St. Peter appeared on the scene in the guise of a beggar and asked him what he was doing. "Making bread," was the reply. St. Peter pondered for a moment and said, "Nay, I shall advise thee better. Give me the incense and I shall give thee whatever thou wishest." Without hesitation Ivan replied that he would take the Saint's flute. The exchange was made, the Saint went off with the incense, and Ivan began to play the flute, whereupon a whole field of cows started dancing. Thereafter Ivan the "fool of God" wandered from village to village playing his flute, and all who heard it—monks, peasants, bears, and nobles —were overwhelmed with a desire to dance.

As the holy fool reveals certain aspects of the Russian religious consciousness, so too does the *stranik** or pilgrim who visited the holy places and sought out holy men to initiate him in the mysteries of the spirit. Pilgrimage has always formed an important part of Russian religious life, and in old Russia there were various types of pilgrims. There were those who set out on a pilgrimage lasting a year or two and then returned to their former lives and work. There were those whose pilgrimages were brief and infrequent, and there were those who became *vechnistraniki* ("eternal pilgrims" or holy wanderers) having renounced the ordinary life of a householder entirely in order to spend their entire lives as wandering pilgrims—and this latter type of pilgrim is more or less unique to Russia.

For the most part the "eternal pilgrims" or holy wanderers have remained anonymous and their sainthood unacclaimed, for they had a quality of seeming not to be different from

---

* Not to be confused with an heretical sect known as the "Straniki" or "Wanderers." These sectarians, like some others known as the Bezsmertniki or "Deathless Ones," wandered eastward either singly or in small groups in order to "escape the kingdom of the Antichrist" and find "the Land of Immortality in the East," invariably only to perish in some isolated section of northeastern Russia.

ordinary sinful men and yet obviously being something very much more. As they were simple, lowly men who were profoundly conscious of sharing in the burden of the world's sin, their sanctity was unobtrusive. This does not mean, however, that it was not recognized, for they were sought as spiritual guides, thaumaturges, and prophets, being greatly revered by laymen and clergy alike.

As with other types of pilgrims, their pilgrimage was sometimes undertaken as a "self-imposed" penance, sometimes as an act of thanksgiving, and sometimes simply as an act of worship or out of a desire for enlightenment. The path followed by the holy wanderers or "eternal pilgrims" involved a natural humility, lowliness, and asceticism rather than discipline. Unlike monks and hermits, they never found it necessary to retire to a monastery or solitary forest hermitage in order to realize salvation in God. As Iulia de Beausobre points out, the monastic state was considered too elevated by many Russians; they preferred greater humility.† The holy wanderers were laymen; they did not take the monastic vows of poverty, chastity, and obedience, but lived the vows without having taken them.

Although most holy wanderers were men, some were women, and occasionally men and women wanderers would travel about together in pairs—a situation which sometimes gave occasion for ridicule or even rebuke among those who, not understanding the purely platonic quality of their relationship,** thought that they were leading a life of licentiousness underneath a mask of sanctity. This rebuke they accepted,

† It is not out of place here to mention the case of the remarkable mystic Alexis Bukharev, who although he did not become a holy wanderer, after many years of monastic life obtained release from his vows and again became a layman. Could one not come out of the angelic abode, he asked, and go in the spirit of Christ's humiliation into the world so as to share in the continuing Divine Kenosis?

** It should be noted that their chastity was not based on a Manichaean abhorrence of the flesh. Rather, it had its basis in the fact that, like monks and nuns, their vocation was chastity and not marriage.

never choosing to defend themselves but preferring to remain silent in their innocence like Christ before His accusers. Indeed, they even welcomed such accusations as a means of partaking in the humiliation of the Godman.

Going from holy place to holy place, from church to church, and from tomb to tomb—from the tomb of St. Sergius at the Monastery of the Holy Trinity near Moscow to the Holy Sepulchre itself—the holy wanderer settled nowhere and had no possessions other than the clothes he was wearing and the knapsack on his back. For sustenance he relied on the charity of others, thus being to his benefactors a means through which they partook of Divine Grace in the mystery of self-giving. His state was one of non-attachment to "the things of this world." If he received no food, he fasted and gave thanks; if he was given a stale crust, an ordinary meal, or invited to a wedding feast, it made no difference to him which, he would eat and joyfully give thanks. He had surrendered himself to the Divine Providence, which he saw manifest in his own life from moment to moment as well as in the lives of others and in the lilies of the fields. And to those whom he encountered during his pilgrimage, he ofttimes quite unknowingly imparted a certain presence of holiness, a holiness which he had absorbed into his person not only through his own sanctity of life but also through frequent contact with holy places, sacred relics, miraculous icons, and the like.

He did not separate himself from the world with all its sin, evil, and sordidness, but like Christ consorted with sinners.

> To the Russian, good and evil are, here on earth, inextricably bound up together. This is, to us, the great mystery of life on earth. Where evil is at its most intense, there also must be the greatest good. To us this is not even an hypothesis. It is axiomatic.[6]
>
> Evil must not be shunned, but first participated in and understood through participation and then through understanding transfigured.[7]

Thus did the holy wanderer choose to remain "in the world." Indeed, on his pilgrimage he came into contact with all elements of society—ordinary peasants, wealthy landowners, thieves, prostitutes, and vagabonds; and to them he came not as a self-righteous reformer, but as a sinful fellow creature. Silently he worshipped the Presence of God within all men, for he perceived the suffering, humiliated Christ within them— even in those in whom the Presence was almost totally obscured through pride and hypocrisy.

Sometimes staying with the lowly in a miserable shack or the most despicable of village inns, sometimes accepting the hospitality of a nobleman, the holy wanderer did not harass his fellow men with trite moral maxims, but listened respectfully to their ordinary conversations—to the stories of their lives, their problems, their joys and their sufferings. The holy wanderer listened and listened, gradually coming to understand the myriad facets of evil and their mysterious relationship with the forces of Light.

Generally he was silent, but when questioned he would tell of churches, monasteries, tombs of saints, and icons of special sanctity which he had seen; he would tell of saints and sinners, of spiritual life and spiritual death, of both common and extraordinary incidents along the road; and if asked for spiritual direction he would give it. "Staying in the world" among the sinful, he realized humility through becoming deeply aware of his own sinfulness and of his sharing in the burden of all men's sinfulness.

Although the Mystical Body of Christ contains saints as well as sinners, it is for the most part a community of ordinary sinners. All men sin, all men are guilty of sinful thought and

St. Ilya (Elijah)—Russian icon

deed, of making an idol of themselves, thereby failing to realize their innermost identity in God. Who can claim sinlessness when all have denied the Christ a thousand times in themselves and in others? There is within Russian spirituality a strongly penitential element. The Jesus Prayer, "Lord Jesus Christ, Son of God, have mercy upon me a sinner," is the endless cry of the Russian heart; and in the Divine Liturgy, the *"Gospodi pomiloi"* (Kyrie eleison) is sung consecutively over and over again, sometimes slowly and sometimes fast, surging and soaring, rising and falling like waves breaking upon the sand, sometimes with a sort of joyous ecstasy and sometimes with gentle supplication, but never with fear or despair. As the Divine Love is the very basis of the cosmos, the mercy of God cannot be doubted‡ although it may take forms which remain veiled and hidden from the understanding of men.

To admit that we are sinful; to develop what one might call "a humility of sinfulness"*; to be aware not only of one's sinfulness and the mutual sharing of all men in each other's guilt but also of the indwelling Christ Who took the sins of the world upon Himself and Whom every man bears within his heart; to love the sinner who gives no explanation of himself, the accused who do not justify themselves, the "scum of the earth," the bruised and the tormented—this is both the way and the fruit of Russian religious experience.

The sins of others are indeed our own through our sharing in a common creaturehood with them, through the unity of all

‡ It may be noted that for centuries there has been current among the Russian peasantry an apocryphal legend wherein the *Bogoroditsa*, the Holy Mother herself, descends into Hell bearing the Divine Love through which she brings deliverance to the damned.

* This should not be confused with an idea once current among certain Russian sectarians, notably the Khlysty with whom the famed "Holy Devil," Rasputin, was affiliated. The Khylsty cultivated sinfulness as a redeeming virtue, deliberately setting out to sin as much as possible "in order to become humble." Needless to say, such a notion was decidedly un-Orthodox.

creatures within their Creator. Thus the burden of an evil deed perpetrated by one individual is not confined to that particular person, but encompasses all men. As long as a man sees himself as separate from his fellow creatures and differentiates between "me" and "you," salvation is impossible. Only with dissolution of egocentricity can union with and identity in God be realized. The individual must become conscious of his "participation" in universal sinfulness, of his own guilt in the sins of his fellow creatures—in every act of pride, hate, violence, and lust ever committed. And in so doing, he must also see the innocence of others, for their sinfulness and responsibility in evil passes from generation to generation, from one person to another, from the whole community of men to one individual, and from one individual to the whole community of men without their willing it, without their desiring it. In a certain sense, the sin of one is the sin of all, but at the same time the holiness of one is the holiness of all. And this is a great mystery, a secret forever hidden in the Wisdom, Love, and Providence of God.

Profoundly aware of evil as evil, the Russian religious consciousness nevertheless sees it as "necessary," for without it the Good would be meaningless. Even that which is most heinously evil occurs only according to the Divine Providence; Judas too had a part to play in the Redemption. However evil a man, some good comes out of his sinfulness, if not for himself, then for others. Even in evil, God can work Good, manifesting His Grace and His Love, bringing men to humility and hence to salvation by means of suffering, a suffering caused by their own sinfulness and the sinfulness of others. In wars and revolutions, in chaos and destruction the "dark side" of the Divine Providence is manifest, manifest out of the infinite Divine Love in order to purify and recreate, to cause awakening and bring salvation to those for whom it is possible. Thus a Russian priest, Father Yuriev, said even of the Russian Revolution with all its bloodshed, chaos, and impiety:

God is no longer speaking in a still small voice! God
is hammering at the door. He is screaming at us in the
market place. God's scream—that is the Revolution!
God's voice—that is the Bolshevik terror. . . .

And there is no use trying to run away . . . Wherever
we run, God's Spirit will overtake us! . . . In the final
analysis this is no doubt the best thing that could happen to us.[8]

In all things, even in the seemingly negative aspects of
life, the secret Wisdom and Providence of God are manifest.
Russian folklore offers ample illustrations of this wholeness
of perception, albeit through the simple and often whimsical
approach of the peasant mind. St. Yuri, for instance, is the
patron of wolves as well as of flocks. He is said to wander
throughout Russia seeing that the flocks get enough to eat, pro-
tecting them from the plague and from wolves. As he is
equally the patron of wolves he also protects them, carries about
a sack of bread to feed them, and sometimes even lets one eat a
sheep when he has run out of his daily supply of bread. In a
somewhat different vein is a legend which relates that Christ
and the Apostles, disguised as pilgrims, were refused even
a stale crust of bread by a rich merchant, but were cheer-
fully fed by an extremely poor widow. Having eaten, they
thanked her and wandered on. As they were walking through
the forest, much to the distaste of the Apostles and above their
protests, Christ enigmatically ordered a wolf to go and kill the
widow's only cow and at the same time caused a barrel of gold
to roll to the rich and unvirtuous merchant's door. The religious Russian does not expect to find justice in this world; he
expects neither a virtuous action to result in material well-
being nor an evil action necessarily to bring about its depri-
vation.

Asceticism plays an important role in Russian religious
life, although it of course means something different to every

religious Russian depending on his status. The rigorous ascetic disciplines of monks and hermits are quite naturally unknown among holy wanderers, "fools in Christ," and ordinary peasant laymen whose asceticism primarily involves a sharing in Christ's humiliation in the world rather than in His forty days of solitude in the wilderness. For the truly religious Russian, asceticism includes far more than fasting, far more than control of the passions of mind and body. Above all else it means imitation of or rather participation in the Divine Kenosis through humiliation, suffering, poverty, and lowliness; it means frank admission of one's own sinfulness, seeing the sins of the world as one's own, and refraining from the judgment of others.

In many respects the average Russian is almost innately ascetic. He is little attached to the "things of this world," and this quality together with his general scorn for money, prestige, and worldly honor perhaps give to his asceticism a certain uniqueness. Not only is it natural and unforced, but this very naturalness tends to check any tendency towards artificial extremes.

There is nothing grim about Orthodox Russian asceticism, for it is not inclined towards excess. With all its stress—in spirit rather than in letter—on the acceptance of suffering, such morbid and unnatural extremes as flagellation remain quite alien to it. Nor is Russian asceticism motivated by any sort of "puritanism." Blinded by a Manichaean concept of the created, the puritan would not have the slightest understanding of the full implication of St. Tikhon Zadonsky's admonition to a self-righteous teetotaler: "Satan too never drinks." Likewise, what puritan would not be scandalized by the gay and festive quality of Sunday—the day of the Resurrection—among Orthodox Russian faithful, and by the joyfulness of most Russian ascetics? The "asceticism" of the puritan is not one which leads to the sanctified state, for being based on self-righteousness it can only lead to a colossal pride. The puritan knows neither joy nor humility; his goal is to deny the divine drama of the cosmos, strip it of its kenotic meaning, and reduce it to something stark and utilitarian. The rags of a beggar are as repugnant to him as the golden vestments of an archbishop, joy and beauty as repellent as suffering and lowliness. Yet, for the Russian ascetic, all these qualities form a harmonious whole, and he loves them all as they proceed from the mysterious Divine Womb. For him, life itself with its suffering and its joy, with all its paradoxes, can in a certain sense be transfigured into an act of worship. Russian asceticism does not lead to a denial of the world, but to an affirmation of it in a very profound sense. In the words of a holy wanderer, "When you see heaven and earth and the sea, and *all* that they contain, be in awe and give praise to their Creator."[9]

The ascetic disciplines of the monks and hermits are rigorous, but they are not meant for everyone. Every man must follow the path of his respective vocation, which may be either lay or monastic. Even those whose path has been one of extreme asceticism seldom have advised others to seek salvation in such a way, unless they were quite sure that such was a necessary part of their vocation. Thus St. Seraphim of Sarov once bade a small group of pilgrims, wearing chains and on their way to Mount Athos to take monastic vows, to throw away their chains and not to go to Athos, rather enigmatically adding that it was not only very difficult there but also intolerably dull.

Toward the lay world, monks and hermits are gently indulgent, realizing that the former is no less according to the Wisdom and Providence of God than their own way of life and that furthermore it is quite necessary for the existence of the monastic order. The relationship between the two is reciprocal; any duality which appears to exist between them is purely superficial.

Russian monks and hermits who have realized a state of perfect sanctity have seldom remained in total reclusion from the outside world, for to borrow the words of Dante: their "desire and will were rolled, even as a wheel which moveth equally, by the Love which moves the sun and the other stars" (*Paradiso* 33). They could not but manifest the Love of God, so they returned to the world or rather let it return to them. Becoming *startsi*,† not only of monks but also of innumerable laymen,** they led others toward salvation and conveyed the mystical insights of the contemplative life to the "outside world." Not discriminating between the spiritual and physical sides of life, they healed the sick in body‡ as well as the sick in soul, offered advice on the myriad problems of daily life, and gave insight into the mysteries of the spirit. So, too, not a few have taken a special delight in feeding bread and apples to bears and children. For them the way of Mary was not incompatible with the way of Martha, but both merged in a single whole.

In the Russian religious consciousness, saints and holy men, however ascetic themselves, are not conceived of as a grim or world-negating group who look with disapproval upon all earthly festivity. Indeed, they are thought to delight in such festivity. A folk tale, for instance, relates that once while a very poor peasant was lamenting the fact that he had nothing to offer his neighbors for the Easter feast, St. Nicolai appeared on the scene in the guise of a holy wanderer. After hearing of the peasant's dilemma, the Saint produced quantities of fresh sturgeon, a huge Easter cake, and then asked the astonished peasant for a sack of dirt which he threw into the well, miraculously turning the water into kvass of unsurpassed goodness.

The process of the sanctification of man through sacra-

† Plural of *starets*—holy elder or spiritual guide.

** Among other Orthodox peoples, this situation has been very infrequent, for the spiritual guidance of the *startsi* has tended to be more or less confined to their monastic brethren.

‡ Not through establishing hospitals or through medical treatment, but rather through the Divine Grace which radiated from the sanctity of their persons.

ments, asceticism, and prayer also involves the sanctification of the cosmos itself—not of the world of appearances, the world of egocentric perception which is subject to the counterfeit dominion of the evil one, but of the real world which "participates" in its Creator and proceeds from the mysterious depths of the Divine Life. The real world is the world perceived by the holy man: a world wherein suffering and joy, ugliness and beauty, and all seeming opposites are seen within a single harmonious whole; a world wherein all things exist through the Divine Love and are guided by the Divine Providence and Wisdom. It is only in the transfiguration of all creation through the realization of the indwelling Presence of God in it that the fulfillment of rigorous asceticism is found. The penitence and fasting of Lent become meaningful only when they culminate in the joy of the Resurrection.

From one point of view the Russian religious consciousness is indeed "otherworldly," but it is not world-negating. There is an abiding consciousness of being deeply rooted in nature and mother earth. "In Mother Earth," writes Fedotov, "converge the most secret and deep religious feelings of the folk. . . . The people venerate with awe the moist black depths, the source of all fertilizing powers, the nourishing breast of nature, and their own last resting place."[10] That the religious Russian rejects all forms of earthly utopianism does not mean that he relegates the holy to something wholly "other." For him, the earth itself is hallowed through the very fact of its being created by God; it is a mystery whose sanctity is realized and ensured through the *Bogoroditsa* or Mother of God, the most holy of all mankind, she through whom the Incarnation took place.

There is in the Russian religious consciousness a profound awareness not only of the indwelling sanctity of the earth, but also of the intimate relationship existing between all creatures, whose reality and innermost identity is found within the fullness of their Creator. Indeed, the Russian psyche possesses an almost innate "wholeness" of perception,* which however receives true and ultimate expression only in a religious context. A holy wanderer writes that the entire "world also seemed to me full of charm and delight. Everything drew me to love and thank God; people, trees, plants, animals. I saw them all as my kinsfolk, I found on all of them the magic of the Name of Jesus."[11] Even the most simple and lowly elements of the cosmos and of daily life take on an almost sacramental aura in the perception of the Russian mystic, who experiences the splendor of the Divine Presence shining forth mysteriously from all things according to the degree in which they exist in God: from the whole cosmos, from himself, from all beings; from the sinner as well as the saint, from the ugly as well as the beautiful; from the stones, the grass, and the earth itself.

It is not out of place to conclude this essay with some excerpts from the discourse of the saintly *starets*, Zossima. Although Zossima is a fictional character created by Dostoyevsky in *The Brothers Karamazov*, he is a faithful embodiment of the Russian holy man and his discourse contains all the warmth and depth of Russian spirituality.

> Brothers, have no fear of men's sin. Love a man even in his sin for that is the semblance of the Divine Love and is the highest love on earth. Love all God's creation, the whole and every grain of sand in it. Love the animals, love the plants, love everything. If you love everything, you will perceive the divine mystery in things. . . . Man, do not pride yourself on superiority to the animals; they are without sin, and you, with your greatness defile the earth. . . .
>
> My brother asked the birds to forgive him; that sounds senseless, but it is right; for all is like an ocean,

* Very revealing of one aspect of this "wholeness" of perception is the Russian word мир (mir), which means "the village community," "the world," "the universe," "union," and "peace."

all is flowing and blending; a touch in one place sets up movement at the other end of the earth. . . .

My friends, pray to God for gladness. Be glad as children, as the birds of heaven. . . . Take yourself and make yourself responsible for all men's sins . . . As soon as you sincerely make yourself responsible for everything and for all men, you will see at once that it is really so. . . .

God took seeds from different worlds and sowed them on this earth, and His garden grew and everything came up that could come up, but what grows lives and is alive only through the feeling of its contact with other mysterious worlds. If that feeling grows weak or is destroyed in you, the heavenly growth will die away in you. . . .

Remember particularly that you cannot be a judge of anyone. For no one can judge a criminal, unless he realizes that he is just such a criminal as the man standing before him. . . . Take upon yourself the crime of the criminal your heart is judging, take it at once, suffer for him yourself, and let him go without reproach. . . .

Love to throw yourself on the earth and kiss it. Kiss the earth and love it with an unceasing, consuming love. Love all men, love everything. Seek that rapture and ecstasy. Water the earth with the tears of your joy and love those tears. Don't be ashamed of that ecstasy, prize it, for it is a gift of God and a great one.[12]

TEACHINGS OF THE HESYCHASTS—
INTRODUCTION

HESYCHASM, "the way of stillness or repose," is the contemplative or mystical tradition of Eastern Orthodox Christianity; it is the Christ-given "initiation" into the Divine mysteries. Its concern is awakening, direct experience of God and deification in Him. In theory, all Orthodox monks and nuns are "hesychasts"; in practice, however, the full hesychast tradition flourishes only in what is perhaps a minority of Orthodox monasteries, notably those where *startsi* of extraordinary holiness and wisdom are present.

For many centuries hesychasm remained chiefly an oral tradition, its teachings forming the subject of direct personal instruction from enlightened elders to their disciples. As time went on, however, more and more hesychast teachings were committed to writing. While today much of hesychasm is to be found in written form,* one often finds hints in hesychast works that the innermost core of the esoteric teachings is, even now, not put to writing; that teachings exist which are known only to the "initiates," to the hesychasts themselves.

In Russia, hesychasm is found among the laity as well as among monks and hermits, but in other Orthodox areas it presupposes entrance into the monastic or hermitic states with their attendant ascetic disciplines and vows, which through transfiguring the passions of the mind and body aid in awaken-

---

* It should be noted that the "spiritual levels" to which hesychast writings relate differ widely and therefore they contain many different and seemingly contradictory points of view. It was assumed that anyone consulting them would have a spiritual director who would have him read only that which was in accord with his "spiritual level."

ing man from his "sleep of death." In the words of St. Gregory Palamas, man "will experience the Divine once the passions of the soul in accord with the body, have been changed and sanctified though not deadened."[1]

Disciplines similar to various forms of Far Eastern yoga play an important part in hesychast life, being utilized as aids to contemplation. For long periods of time, increasing in length as he becomes more adept, the hesychast remains completely quiescent in a darkened room, sitting either cross-legged on the floor or on a low stool symbolizing the dung hill upon which Job sat, his hands either in an attitude of prayer or with one over the heart while the other holds a rosary, his eyes focused on his navel while he repeats the Jesus Prayer, constantly invoking the Sacred Name of Jesus† in conjunction with his heartbeat and respiration.

When the hesychast awakens "a new faith is born, not opposed to the first faith, but confirming it,"[2] writes St. Isaac of Syria. The mystical teachings of the hesychasts have arisen out of the revealed Tradition, in which they are firmly based. Indeed, it might be said that the "exoteric" and mystical are mutually complementary aspects of the Sacred Tradition as a whole. Each is, in a certain sense, dependent on the other, and between them there is constant interaction.

Hesychasm is not something imperative upon all the Orthodox faithful, but from the spiritual energy and transfiguring light which radiates from Orthodoxy's contemplative mystics,

† See Essay IV for the significance and place of the Sacred Name in Orthodox mysticism.

Simopetra Monastery—Mount Athos, Greece
(Courtesy M. Hatzis)

the whole of Orthodoxy finds vitality and strength. In its fullest form hesychasm is reserved for those whose vocation is the "vision of God" here and now in the contemplative state. Hence care must be taken by the ordinary layman not to draw from hesychasm "a distorted wisdom." Callistus Xanthopoulos, a fourteenth-century Patriarch of Constantinople, says of hesychast teachings, "If they hear this, let none of the uninitiated or those who still 'have need of milk' touch it, for this is something forbidden to touch before its time."[3] The chief danger lies in the creation of a false duality between the "exoteric" and the mystical elements of the Sacred Tradition.

When the mystical is separated from the total unity of the Tradition and is set up over and above theology, sacred rites, and "externals," thus becoming sectarian and anti-traditional, it is false. However valid the mystical teachings are within the context of the whole, they lose their validity when separated from it and lead only into ignorance and confusion. Let it be clear that there is not and cannot be any hesychasm outside the Church or in any way separated from it.**

During the fourteenth century the orthodoxy of certain hesychast teachings was called into question in Byzantium by a small but powerful group who were the proponents of an anti-mystical, neo-latinist scholasticism. Drawing their arguments from the writings of Thomas Aquinas, the neo-latinist theologians declared that many hesychast teachings were heretical. Cries of "pantheism," "Gnosticism," and "blasphemy" were wrongfully raised against the hesychasts, and it was thus that hesychasm, which is not concerned with theological subtleties but with awakening and the "vision of God," was forced to

** This is not to say that "equivalents" of hesychasm do not exist in other spiritual traditions. Many interesting parallels may be found in the contemplative tradition of Western Christianity, in Sufism, in Hasidism, in the japa yoga of the Hindus, and in various aspects of Pure Land and Zen Buddhism.

justify its orthodoxy. This task fell chiefly to St. Gregory Palamas,‡ Archbishop of Thessalonika and former monk of Mount Athos, who presented a brilliant exposition and clarification of hesychasm. Needless to say, the complete orthodoxy of all hesychast teachings was acknowledged by the Patriarch and Synod, who declared the views of the neo-latinists heretical, although not without considerable opposition by the Byzantine Empress. With this final triumph of hesychasm, its mystical teachings found new affirmation, and Western scholasticism and rationalism were rejected forever by the Orthodox Church.

Although hesychasm strictly speaking is not to be equated with certain necessary theological formulations which have arisen out of it, thus giving intellectual and theological form to its inner mystical experience, neither can it be properly understood apart from these theological formulations. Indeed, the latter form an integral part of the total complex of hesychasm and serve as a safeguard against a distorted understanding of the hesychast perception of reality by the "non-initiate."

While hesychasm lays considerable stress on the immanence of God, immediate "vision" of Him, and the possibility of the creature's deification in Him, one must be careful not to misunderstand it as some sort of Christian pantheism—for this it very definitely is not. It is possible, however, to say that hesychasm is, in a certain sense, "panentheistic." God indwells man, reveals Himself to man, and is immanent in all creation, which He in a certain sense includes within Himself; all existing things "participate" in Him. In the words of St. Gregory Palamas, "God is named the nature of all existing things because they participate in Him and are formed by

‡ St. Gregory Palamas died in 1359 and was canonized in 1368, being designated by the Church as "the last and greatest of the Fathers." He is commemorated twice during the liturgical year—on the Sunday following the Feast of the Triumph of Orthodoxy and on the date of his death, November 14.

participation in Him."[4] Thus God is called the "Being of all that exists and the All of all things." This "participation" of creature in Creator, however, is not in the least pantheistic, for a clear distinction is maintained between Uncreated (God) and created. The creature partakes of God, exists in God and through God, but always remains creature even when union with and deification in God the Uncreated is realized. Thus St. Gregory Palamas states, "We partake of the divine nature, and yet at the same time we do not partake of it at all."[5] In other words, while creation is dependent upon God and finds the fullness of its reality only within Him through being "raised by Divine Grace" into full participation in the Divine Nature, God is dependent upon nothing and is real within Himself. "Participation in God" does not involve being "a part" of Him, but rather not existing outside of or apart from Him. If God was removed from creation, the latter would have no reality.

Characteristic of hesychasm is the assertion on one hand of God's "transcendental and 'extra-universal' nature" and on the other of "His self-revelation to and immanent and real presence in the world."[6] Infinitely transcendent or "beyond every name that can be named and everything that can be thought,"[7] God is at the same time fully present or immanent in all creation. One and indivisible, both Unity and Trinity, both hidden and revealed, both unmanifest and manifest, God reveals Himself as being and in terms of being—and at the same time is "above" or beyond being. Before God, the ultimate Mystery Uncreated and Eternal, we cannot but say with certainty and humility: "Holy God, Holy Strong One, Holy Deathless One, have mercy upon us."

TEACHINGS OF THE HESYCHASTS

"Awake thou that sleepest and arise from the dead."
Eph. 5:14
"Who am I and who says that I am somebody?"
St. Barsanuphius

"IN PEOPLE in their ordinary state," writes Bishop Ignati, "the spirit, struck by the Fall, sleeps an unwakable sleep identical with death."[8] All hesychast discipline and contemplation is directed toward "remembering God" and awakening from "the sleep of death"—also known as the state of prelest—through "collecting the mind within the heart" as the center of immediate knowledge.

What is prelest?* Paraphrasing Bishop Ignati, Kadloubovsky defines it as "the corruption of human nature through the acceptance by man of mirages mistaken for truth; we are all in prelest."[9] Prelest is the resulting state of man's "wandering" from the *Istina* or Absolute Truth and it has its basis in his fallen or egocentric† nature, which through sundering his inner wholeness causes "forgetfulness of God," obscures the splendorous Divine Presence, and creates a multitude of illusions which infect his very perception of the cosmos. Nicephorus the Hermit states that "it happens to us as to Adam," who

---

* The Russian word "прелесть" (prelest) is the term used to translate the Greek "πλάνη," which means "wandering" or "going astray" (cf. "πλάνος"—"deceiver" or "impostor"). In old Russian "prelest" chiefly denoted a state of enchantment, charm, or illusion, and had the various connotations of "captivity," "seduction," "dispersion," "artfulness," and "cunning."

† It should be noted that throughout these essays the term "egocentric" or "self-centered" is used as a synonym for the fallen state and as the opposite of "Theocentric" or "God-centered." By the former is meant "self-centered" in the purely negative sense, that is, self-centered "without God." Actually, one might say that the holy man too is self-centered. He, however, is self-centered in God.

by associating with the serpent and trusting the serpent's counsel, "tasted of the forbidden fruit and was utterly filled with prelest."[10]

Not only does "prelest" denote man's "wandering from God," but also the illusions which are attendant on and manifestations of this state. Enchanted and captivated by "the phantoms of prelest," man becomes blind to God the Divine Center, to the true nature of all creation, and to his true or real self. According to Theophan the Hermit, forms of prelest "stupify a man and abduct him from his own self."[11] "The mind," he says, "runs after this fantasy like a child attracted by a skillful juggler."[12]

Through contemplation, detached observation of his inner state, and constant invocation of the Sacred Name, the hesychast discerns the "various forms of prelest, the different wiles, the incredible subterfuges";[13] and by means of this discernment he begins to awaken from illusion and realize his "nothingness."

"In our incomprehensible self-deception," writes Theophan the Hermit, "we do not cease to believe that we are something, and something not unimportant. . . . Realize your nothingness."[14] "Having realized your nothingness, you will learn many great and marvelous things,"[15] states St. Maximus the Confessor. The realization of one's "nothingness" involves liberation from the illusions and dispersion of the egocentric state, vision from within God, and participation in the Divine Nature; it involves the birth of "selflessness" and true humility. We, however, who regard ourselves as "something" or "somebody" and seek to affirm our existence not within God in Whom every created being finds his wholeness and reality, but rather within ourselves as isolated individual egos, remain enslaved to a world of illusion and blind to the true nature of reality both created and Uncreated. "Trusting the serpent's counsel," we, in our egocentrism, project our inner state upon the cosmos. We see all things in terms of our own inner dispersion and perceive

all men as self-contained individual beings external not only to
God but also to one another and to ourselves. Thus deluded,
we fail to experience creation as it exists in the Spirit of God,
for we see everything as "external" to ourselves. But actually
there is no "external world"; other beings are not external to
us—neither the living nor the dead, neither the holy nor the
unholy—for within the Spirit of God all created things exist in
each other and "support" each other. So, too, within the Mystical Body all men exist in intimate relationship with one another. "There is one body, for we are all members of his body,
of his flesh, and of his bones,' " states Patriarch Callistus. "Let
the initiated hearken to these words!"[16]

In order to awaken from the illusions and bondage of
prelest, man must return to his primordial state of wholeness
and sanctity,** to the simple purity and non-dual Theocen-
trism of his original nature before the Fall, through entering
deeply within himself. In the words of Nicephorus the Hermit,
"It is impossible for us to become reconciled and united with
God, if we do not first return to ourselves, as far as it lies in
our power, or if we do not enter within ourselves."[17] Enshrined
in the depths of the heart of every man is the resplendent
Divine Indwelling. "Enter your inner treasure-house and you
will see the treasure-house of heaven. For both one and the
other are the same,"[18] writes St. Isaac of Syria. "The kingdom
of Heaven, nay rather, the King of Heaven . . . is within us,"[19]
states St. Gregory Palamas.

Becoming receptive to the Hagia Sophia or Divine Wisdom which, although dormant within him due to the Fall,
remains inherent in the depths of his being, the hesychast
perceives the mysterious flame of Godhead ever present within

** Deification itself, according to Orthodox theology, actually involves
more than return to the primordial state before the Fall, for it also
involves acquiring a "fullness" of sanctity and participation in the Divine
Nature which man did not possess even before the Fall.

him. Through Divine Grace, he begins to awaken from illusion and directly experience the Divine mysteries as God reveals Himself in the silent depths of his heart. Saying with the Theotokos, who is termed the "first hesychast," "Be it unto me according to Thy Word," he in a certain sense gradually becomes like unto her, she who is the most perfect of all creatures—Godbearer and "creaturely aspect of the Hagia Sophia." The all-consuming flame of Divinity begins to grow and leap within him, finally culminating in his deification. Likewise, he comes to realize that any virtue which he may seem to possess is not his own and does not originate in his individual "I," but rather is dependent upon the Grace of God and originates in Him.

Before the hesychast awakens to the indwelling Deity, however, he must face the inner darkness within himself—"Do not wish only to perceive within yourself the divine light, and spiritual joys and sweetnesses, but also darknesses."[20] The hesychast must meet the most sinful of the sinful within himself; he must see the devil with clarity of vision, come face to face with the demons which lurk within the dark side of his heart, and realize that the most depraved thoughts and actions ever thought or committed are not external to himself. The inner darknesses must be recognized for what they are, for with clear and careful discernment of them they lose their power to enter into the "inner chamber of the heart" and cause spiritual death. In the words of Hesychius of Jerusalem, the hesychast "is not ashamed of his enemies—unclean demons walking round [within] him, but speaks 'with the enemies in the gate.' "[21] Similarly, St. Abba Dorotheus says, "Know that if a man is attacked by some thought . . . and does not acknowledge it, he only strengthens it against himself."[22]

According to hesychast teaching, awakening and deification in God occur "without thought." The mind must become free from the continuous maze of thoughts, words, memories, and fantasies which "keep it asleep." Indeed, "quietness of mind" is of primary importance in the whole process of inward transfiguration. St. Isaac of Syria writes that the wisdom bestowed by Divine power from within "manifests and reveals itself in the innermost depths of the soul itself, immaterially, suddenly, spontaneously and unexpectedly. . . . It does not feed hope with any image in advance, nor can its coming be observed: but within the image imprinted in the hidden mind, it reveals itself by itself, *without thought*."[23] St. Basil the Great states that God does not "dwell in any imaginings or mental structures which present themselves and surround the corrupt soul like a wall, so that it is powerless to look at truth, directly, but continues to cling to mirrors."[24] And according to St. Gregory of Sinai, prolixity of mind "deprives man of essential wisdom, true contemplation and the knowledge of the one and indivisible."[25]

In a certain sense, man's "forgetfulness of God," inner dispersion and all the other conditions attendant on the state of prelest have their origin in and are sustained by thoughts. "The evil one, being mind without body, cannot lead souls astray except by means of imagination and thoughts,"[26] writes Hesychius of Jerusalem. "The mind can make no progress . . . if it does not put the inner man in order by stopping thoughts turning round and round. For such a man's inner eye is always blind."[27] The thoughts of the hesychast, he states, must not be allowed "to attach themselves to the suggested image (which arises in the mind) or to fraternize and allow it to multiply or to identify with it."[28] Similarly Patriarch Callistus defines the purpose of various hesychast yoga practises as "teaching the mind, under the influence of this natural method, to abandon its usual circling, captivity and dispersion and to return to attention to itself; and through such attention to reunite with itself."[29]

This "circling, captivity, and dispersion" which causes "forgetfulness of God" has its basis in attachment to and identification with the images which arise in the mind, in "thoughts which leave imprints." "The thought of God is not to be found in those thoughts which imprint images in the mind," writes Abba Evagrius, "but in the thoughts which make no imprints."[30]‡ It is not out of place here to mention an anecdote related in the *Philokalia* which affords some insight into the above. It is said that once while a certain abbot was delivering a discourse to the monks of his monastery, two poisonous snakes suddenly appeared crawling towards him. In no way perturbed, he remained unharmed by simply arching the soles of his feet and letting the snakes pass through.

Many are the ways in which man's mental vision becomes distorted, and of these one of the chief is the result of failure to realize that the past events of one's life have ceased to be; to paraphrase Theoleptus, they were but as footsteps on the snow which have either been washed away by the rains or have melted in the rays of the sun. Yet, we who remain in the "sleep of death" continue to cling to past memories and consort with the phantoms of prelest. "In the soul of the negligent, evil spirits raise memories of his parents, brothers, relatives, and friends, as well as of banquets . . . and they incite him to meet the former and take part in the latter with eyes, tongue, and body; so that he uselessly wastes the present,"[31] writes Theoleptus.

Our involvement with and attachment to the images which arise within the ordinary mind prevent "the hidden mind"* from functioning and cause its faculty for direct perception of "the one and indivisible" to remain dormant. Thus blinded by egocentric illusion, the mind continues in its "sleep of death." Only when it is purified and returns to its "natural state of health" wherein the "secret wisdom of the hidden mind" per-

‡ Or one might say, thoughts which "do not stick in the mind."

* Care should be taken not to confuse "the hidden mind" with the "unconscious" or "subconscious" of psychology. The two have nothing in common.

meates all mental "activity" does liberation from the illusions
of the fallen state occur. The dispersion, attachment, disorder,
and circling of the egocentric mind give way to the tran-
quility and wholeness of the Theocentric mind. With this liberation from the duality and illusion of prelest, thought as we
know it ceases. This, of course, does not mean that the mind
becomes vacant. Indeed, Hesychius of Jerusalem states that "if
the heart is completely freed of fantasies, it begins to give birth
to Divine and mysterious thoughts, which play within it as
fishes play and dolphins leap in a calm sea."[32] The "thought"
or condition of mind of the holy man who has "returned" to the
primordial and sanctified state that existed before the Fall is
unaware and spontaneous, for he has no "separate awareness"
of himself and he dwells in constant "remembrance of God."
In his every "thought" "the thought of God" is present, for he
perceives nothing outside the vision of God, apart from Him,
or apart from the totality of His creation. All that arises in his
mind flows freely through it without obscuring his immediate
perception of "the one and indivisible."

Closely related to the mental state of non-attachment is
the realization that the natural condition of the created is one of
constant flux; creation is a continual process, as also is decay.
St. Isaac of Syria states that every "being suffers changes without number, and every man is different from hour to hour."[33]
Failing to realize the evanescent, constantly changing quality of
all things as well as the fact that nothing in the entire realm
of created being has an independent reality apart from God
and the totality of His creation, we "wander in darkness . . .
clutching with both hands at nothing,"[34] to use the words of
St. Maximus the Confessor. Indeed, as long as we cling to the
illusionary world of our egocentric perception, we remain in a
state of "forgetfulness of God." Thus Bishop Ignati writes,
"One living a recollected life should not stare at anything, and
should not listen to anything with special diligence, but should
see as if without seeing and hear as if in passing, so that the

memory and power of attention may always be free."[35] As the mind becomes purified of all illusion, the hesychast gains immediate knowledge of the constant flux of all things. Thus he perceives the created and temporal as it exists within God; and at the same time he sees "beyond" the constant flux of the created and temporal to the Uncreated and Eternal, although in no way negating the former.

The process of a man's inward transfiguration which, according to Theophan the Hermit, occurs "unnoticeably, without ostentation, as is the case with the growth of a body,"[36] is gradual in nature. As the hesychast "grows" in sanctity through Divine Grace, the passions of the mind and body are transformed and he gradually becomes "dead to himself," "dead to his fallen nature." Only then does what may be variously described as "rebirth," "awakening," and "deification" occur. "Deification," writes St. Gregory Palamas, "lifts him who is deified outside himself."[37] The entire Godhead is contained in him, and he in It. Thus he suffers "a change in his mental vision," states St. Simeon Neotheologos, "for he will be unable to imagine anything . . . and will see only God in all things."[38] Having awakened from the sleep of death, ignorance, and illusion, the hesychast perceives the Uncreated Divine Light of the Transfiguration, "the glory of God" which knows no bounds in either time or space. "The Light of the Transfiguration of our Lord," writes St. Gregory Palamas, "neither comes into being nor ceases to be and cannot be circumscribed."[39] The Transfiguration of Christ on Mount Tabor actually involved no change in the Person of Christ, but rather a change in the consciousness or awareness of the disciples. It revealed what always was, is, and shall be—not only in the Person of Christ, who being God is the Source of the Light, but also in the entirety of creation which always remains overshadowed by and enshrouded in the Light and Glory of its Creator, the One in Whom it finds its wholeness, reality, and innermost identity. In the Uncreated Light the Kingdom of God and His immediate Presence are revealed.

Boundless and ever present, the Divine Light, which in a certain sense encloses within itself both light and darkness, is not present to a greater or lesser degree in different times and places, but rather remains present to the same degree everywhere whether or not it is perceived. Enveloping all things within itself, it nevertheless remains "subjectively" unmanifest to us whose awareness of reality is blinded by prelest. One might say that the Uncreated Light is hidden from most men much in the same way that the sun is hidden from the blind. St. Gregory Palamas writes, "The Divine energy† [the Uncreated Light] and the grace of the Spirit which is present everywhere and inseparable from Him, is incommunicable and as though absent for those who are unable to commune with it on account of their impurity."[44] In the words of Father Krivosheine, "What changes is not the Light, but our capacity to

† In Orthodox mystical theology, the Uncreated Light is spoken of as one of the "Divine energies" "by which out of His unmanifested and hidden state, God manifests Himself to the world, exteriorizing Himself."[40]

It may be noted that Orthodoxy makes a distinction between the "Divine Super-substance" which may in a certain sense be equated with the transcendental, hidden, unmanifest "aspect" of God as He is in Himself, and the "Uncreated Divine energies" or "energy" which may in a certain sense be equated with the immanent, manifest "aspect" of God. One must be careful not to construe this distinction as some sort of duality within the Divine Nature. St. Gregory Palamas states that "when we name the one God, we name all that is God, both substance and energy."[41] According to Father Krivosheine the distinction between the two "is, at the same time, their indivisible unity."[42] Similarly, the Council of 1351 stated, "Neither does the unity destroy the difference, nor the difference contradict the unity."[43]

St. Alexei of Moscow—Russian icon

apprehend It."[45] "If the mind . . . is in its natural state of health," writes St. Isaac of Syria, "it clearly sees the glory of Christ; it does not question, does not have to learn, but delights in the mysteries of the new world."[46]

Experience of the Uncreated Light of the Divine Transfiguration is "a genuine perceptual apprehension. . . . The ascetic, now united to God and made effectually 'a partaker of the Divine Nature' (2 Peter I:4) *sees* the Divine Glory in and about him, as the disciples were permitted to see it in Christ at the Transfiguration."[47] This state of perception "has nothing to do with 'ecstasies' or 'raptures' or 'visions.' . , . On the contrary, it is the ordinary, normal, permanent state of those who live in constant union with God. . . . Their 'senses discover the infinite in everything,' and they move open-eyed where most men are blind."[48]

The Uncreated Light is both an inward illumination and an outward radiance; it is manifest both from within and from without; it is experienced by the whole being of the holy man who perceives it, and is seen with both the physical eyes and with the "inner eye of the Spirit." Being that "Light" which is God, it is the exteriorization of His invisible Presence, and perception of it is the "sign" or manifestation of the interior transfiguration which occurs when man becomes "whole" in God and present in the fullness of His Spirit. An incident from the life of St. Seraphim of Sarov perhaps gives some insight into the above. It is related that one winter while St. Seraphim was chopping wood as the snow fell gently to the earth, he was visited by his disciple, the blessed Motovilov, who questioned him about the ever-present Spirit of God. Suddenly St. Seraphim laid down his ax and grasped Motovilov firmly by the shoulders.

"At this moment, my friend, we are both in the Spirit of God," said Seraphim.

"Father!" cried Motovilov, "your eyes flash lightnings, your face is more dazzling than the sun."

"Rejoice, God-loving one." said the Saint. "I too behold

such light in you. At this moment, you have become present in the fullness of the Spirit of God."[49]

Within the Uncreated Light, a whole "new world" is hidden—a world enshrouded in the Mystery and Presence of its Creator and Manifestor, however much removed from its original primordial or paradisal state it has become. "The expressions which describe the Light," states Father Krivosheine, "designate now God Himself . . . [and] now the inward state of the one who apprehends Him . . . in a certain sense, these two are the same."[50] The world is to us what we inwardly are. He who is "in prelest," whose soul is in a state of dispersion, and whose heart is "at war with itself" remains blind to God and to the world as it exists in God. All of his perceptions correspond to the disunity of his inner state, and for him the entire cosmos is Hell. But for the holy man "whose heart is filled with . . . the Holy Spirit, wherever he may be, everywhere will be Paradise because the Kingdom of Heaven is within us."[51] Inwardly "recollected" and one with God, he directly experiences the "one and indivisible" and, in the words of St. Isaac of Syria, *"through grace receives into himself the new world, that is not multiple. . . .* When mind is renewed and heart sanctified, then all the apprehensions, which arise in a man correspond to the nature of the world he enters."[52] Having "died to himself" and hence to the dispersion and duality of the "old world," the holy man awakens to Life in God and to the cosmos as it exists in the Spirit of God—a Theocentric cosmos radiant with the Uncreated Light, a cosmos shining with the splendor, mystery, and life of its Creator. Even the ofttimes rather dour St. Anthony the Hermit writes, "There is no place and no substance where God is not present. . . . A God-loving man knows beyond doubt that nothing exists without God, that He is everywhere and in all things."[53]

Living in constant "remembrance of God," Who is totally without opposites, and always aware of His all-pervading Presence, the holy man perceives the innermost Divine content of all creatures. He neither discriminates between men nor condemns anyone, for having realized true humility as well as knowing that man's "freewill is bound,"[54] he is "above blaming and accusing any man."[55] St. Isaac of Syria asks, "How can one say that a man has attained purity?—when he sees all men as being good, and when none appears to him to be unclean or defiled—then he is indeed pure in heart."[56]

Sinless and free from all evil himself, the holy man nevertheless sees sin, evil, and all the seemingly negative aspects of life in their proper perspective from within the Wisdom of God. He perceives the Light which shines in darkness even where evil is at its most intense; he knows that good can emerge from evil and that chaos, destruction, and suffering can serve to stir man from his "sleep of death" and awaken him to ultimate reality. Even so, it must not be thought that he remains insensitive and unmoved by the cruelty, violence, bloodshed, and other evils suffered by the creatures of God. St. Isaac of Syria writes that the heart of a holy man "embraces the whole of creation—men, birds, animals, demons, and every kind of creature," and so great is his love for them that "he cannot bear to see or hear any pain or sorrow caused to any creature."[57] Rejoicing with God and all who rejoice in Him, the holy man also suffers with God and all who suffer in Him. At all times he is filled with love and compassion for all creatures, and even on those rare occasions when a holy man has manifested the "Divine Wrath" in some minor form of violence—as did the Godman Himself when He seized a whip and drove the money-changers from the temple—the boundless Love of God has been present.

Holy men, however, do not conform to any one pattern of character and behavior. Each manifests the Wisdom and Love of God according to his individual temperament, background, and gifts. Some are severe and others are lenient, some are of a very joyous nature and others are not. According to a story which illustrates this point with considerable insight, there were once two *startsi* who resided in monasteries not too far apart, but who had never met. Each was said to be a saint who radiated the Divine Presence; each was noted for his holiness of life and his healing and prophetic powers; each was daily visited by many pilgrims, penitents, and seekers of Divine mysteries. Yet, these two *startsi* were very different from one another. One was of a very severe nature and ate nothing but dried bread and a soup made from bitter weeds. To those who sought his spiritual guidance his counsel was long and he always made it a point to impress upon the penitents the gravity of what seemed to them to be but the least of their sins. He was serene of countenance but was never known to smile, and he frequently imposed penances. The other *starets*, quite lacking in severity, was of a quiet and joyous nature. Every year he made it a point to taste of every fruit, vegetable, and cheese available in order to rejoice in the goodness of God's creation. He greeted penitents with the words, "Joy, Christ is risen," listened to their confessions in silence, and dismissed them with a blessing without ever imposing a penance even for the gravest of sins.

One day at exactly the same time, both *startsi* happened to overhear the conversations of some pilgrims to their respective monasteries. The severe *starets* heard one pilgrim tell another: "The *starets* here is not even joyful. He acts as though the Great Lent lasted through the whole year—and the way he exaggerates even the slightest of sins! You should see the *starets* at the other monastery. He is a real holy man, radiant with the joy of the Resurrection and the Presence of God." At the same time in his monastery, the joyful *starets* overheard a pilgrim say, "The *starets* here hardly ever utters a word. Never any advice on how to avoid sin, never a penance even for the worst of sins. If you ask me, he is entirely too joyful and doesn't have a proper sense of sin. It is plain to see that his fasting isn't very strenuous, and I've even heard it said that he eats raisin cakes offered by pilgrims and penitents. What kind of a holy man is this? You should see the *starets* at the other monastery. He only eats stale bread and weed soup—and he is so emaciated from his ascetic life that the winds could carry him right up into the heavens. Now, there is a true holy man."

And simultaneously each *starets* was overwhelmed with the desire to go and pay his respects to the other. Both setting out from their monasteries, they encountered each other along the road, each recognizing the other as the one whom he sought. They immediately fell prostrate before each other, blessed each other in silence, and then returned to their respective monastries.

"God's will is an immutable law for all that is and will be,"[58] states Theophan the Hermit. "All things happening to us happen according to God's will . . . although we cannot suppose that some things such as our sins are a direct result of a willed action of God's, yet even they do not happen without God's leave."[59] In the clarity of his Theocentric vision, the holy man knows that nothing occurs outside the Wisdom of God, that all that has been, all that is, and all that will be is in accord with the mysterious and inscrutable Divine Providence, the ways of which far exceed the rational understanding of men.

As he has "surrendered himself to the Divine Providence," he realizes "repose in God" and is freed from all anxiety. The enlightened, says St. Isaac of Syria, "are no longer so shameless as to return in their prayers to their former petitions: 'Give us this' or 'Take away that,' and they have no care for themselves. For at each moment, by the spiritual eyes of faith, they see the Fatherly Providence."[60] Theophan the Hermit writes:

> Plunge with eyes closed into the sea of Divine Providence and benevolence; let the mighty waves of God's will carry you. . . . As a result you will always enjoy freedom and, tied to nothing from any side, will always rejoice and be at peace with yourself. This freedom

of the spirit . . . is nothing but a steady abiding of the inner man in himself. . . . Thus free, you will be partaking of that divine and inexpressable joy, which is inseparable from the kingdom of God established within us.[61]

Becoming one with the Divine Nature, the holy man realizes true, absolute, and abiding freedom. Free from the sinfulness and illusion of the fallen state, he "rises above the summit of the Law" and is liberated from its "yoke." True virtue flows forth from him effortlessly, spontaneously, and naturally without any recourse to laws or commandments, for all his perceptions, thoughts, and actions are in accord with his sanctified state. "When the power of the Spirit has penetrated," writes St. Isaac of Syria, "then, in place of the law of the Scriptures . . . a man is secretly taught by the Spirit."[62]

Thus sanctified, he receives "the peace which passeth all understanding." "God is the beginning, the middle, and the end of all that is," states St. Maximus the Confessor, "the beginning, as Creator, the middle, as Provider, the end, as the Consummator, for, as the scriptures say, 'of him, and through him, and to him, are all things.' "[63]

NOTE

It may be observed that the eschatological process of transfiguration bears many parallels with and helps to clarify the meaning of the transfiguration of the holy man and his perception of the cosmos through awakening and deification in God.

As an eschatological event, the transfiguration of the cosmos involves the metamorphosis of "this world" into a "new world." Constantly all things move towards their dissolution. As the age proceeds man falls deeper and deeper into the ignorance, illusion, and duality of prelest, although within this general decline there are brief periods of spiritual renaissance in which the tendency to become progressively worse seems to be reversed. These brief periods are, however, always followed by even greater plunges into the abysses of darkness. Yet, as the world moves towards its dissolution, so too it moves towards consummation, transfiguration, and renewal in God—toward the *apocatastasis** or "restoration of the Garden of Eden," a restoration of things as they were in the beginning. In short, the *apocatastasis* involves "a return" to the original primordial state of holiness before the Fall. This transfiguration, however, occurs only with the destruction and end of "this world." a happening which coincides with the "second coming," "universal resurrection" and "last judgment."

The reign of Christ and the transfiguration of the world are immediately preceded by the final period of man's spiritual decline which culminates in the seeming triumph of the forces of darkness and evil in the person of the Antichrist. While outwardly appearing to be good, "the reign of the Antichrist" is inwardly intensely evil. It is a subtle counterfeit of the "reign of Christ," and is indeed the supreme manifestation of Satanic deception. Only with the appearance of Christ and the manifestation of the "Divine Wrath" in which God assumes, as it were, His function as "Destroyer" does the reign of evil end as does the world itself—that is, the world as we know it. Yet, destruction and extinction are followed by creation and renewal. Thus with the death of "this world," the "new world" is born. Only then shall there be a literal and universal restoration of the primordial state and a renewal and transfiguration of all things in God.

In many respects, the whole process of transfiguration in the holy man follows the same pattern as the process of the eschatological transfiguration—and certain very definite similarities can be observed between the two. Both involve the extinction or death of "the old" and the emergence of "the new" which in both cases is seen as "a return" to the primordial state of sanctity and wholeness. Both mark the end of the reign of evil through libera-

---

* It should be noted that this in no way implies certain theories alien to Orthodox Christian Tradition which Origen associated with the *apocatastasis*.

tion from the illusion and duality of the fallen state. Indeed, it might be said that the process involved in the inward transfiguration of the holy man, in a certain sense, reflects or prefigures on a microcosmic scale certain events which shall be manifest on a macrocosmic scale in the eschatological process. For instance, the holy man's "dying to himself" quite clearly reflects the eschatological event of "the end of this world." Similarly, his subsequent deification and perception of "the new world which is not multiple" clearly reflect the *apocatastasis.*

THE INVOCATION OF THE SACRED NAME—
INTRODUCTION

"Pray without ceasing."
I Thes. 5:17
*"We will walk, O Lord, in the light of the glory of
Thy countenance and in Thy Name will we rejoice unto
all ages. Alleluia."*

Troparion for the Feast of the
Transfiguration of the Saviour

No ELEMENT of hesychast practice is of greater significance
than the Jesus Prayer, which is also known as the invocation of
the Name of Jesus and the Prayer of the Heart. Although its
commonest form is "Lord Jesus Christ, Son of God, have mercy
upon me a sinner," it may ultimately be reduced to just one
word—*"Isus"* or "Jesus," the Sacred Name itself. The latter is
said to be the most ancient form, and many devotees deem it
best by virtue of its simplicity. Regardless of what form is
used, the heart and core of the Jesus Prayer is the Sacred Name.

All Orthodox monks and nuns are given a rosary of one
hundred beads during the solemn rites of profession with the
words, "Receive, brother (sister), the sword of the Spirit, which
is the Word of God. Carry it on your lips, in your mind, and
in your heart, and say unceasingly: 'Lord Jesus Christ, Son of
God, have mercy upon me a sinner.' " The Sacred Name may
be repeated either verbally or mentally. The beginner always
starts with verbal invocation, which, however, may be silent as
long as the tongue pronounces the word or words in the mouth.
Gradually this gives way to mental invocation, finally becoming
"the silent Prayer of the Heart" as deification is realized. "Continue constantly in the name of the Lord Jesus that the heart
may swallow the Lord and the Lord the heart, and that these
two may be one,"[1] writes Bishop Ignati. "Whether talking,

sitting, walking, making something, eating, or occupied in some other way," states Patriarch Callistus, "one should at all times and in every place call upon the name of God."[2]

The cult of the Sacred Name has remained one spiritual way among others in the total complex of Eastern Orthodox spirituality. Hermits have existed, however, for whom the invocation of the Sacred Name was, one might say, the sole spiritual way. Living alone in the vast forests of northern Russia, a hundred or more miles from the nearest village, isolated even from the rites of the Church, many hermits knew no other spiritual way than that of the Sacred Name. No matter what he was doing—chopping wood, picking berries, bowing before his icon, or applying herbs to the injured paw of a bear he had saved from a hunter's trap—from the hermit's lips issued no other sound and within his heart was no other movement than the Sacred Name, *Isus*.

It should be noted that it is only among the Russians that the invocation of the Sacred Name ever gained wide currency among the laity. For other Orthodox peoples, such as the Greeks, its use is almost entirely confined to monks, nuns, and hermits. Spreading among the Russian laity and adapted to the Russian lay mind, the monastic hesychasm of Greece and the Near East quite naturally underwent many transformations. The Jesus Prayer was its sole vehicle. Russian laymen and indeed many Russian clergy and monks had no knowledge of and no interest in Byzantine mystical theology. Their approach was primarily devotional. So, too, the various external aids and disciplines utilized by monks and hermits in conjunction with unceasing repetition of the Jesus Prayer were modified to meet the needs of the layman. Russian lay devotees of the Name adopted the use of the rosary, but the severe ascetic and yogic disciplines proper to monks and hermits were, of course, impracticable for them, whether they were peasant farmers or wandering pilgrims. Whereas a modified form of hesychast yoga was practiced by some Russian laymen, it was not considered indispensable, and many devotees arose who said that while these yogic disciplines might be an aid to concentration for some, they were a hindrance for others and by no means were a necessary adjunct to the invocation of the Sacred Name. Thus unhampered by the disciplines associated with it in the monasteries, the Jesus Prayer spread among the Russian laity, thereby opening a way of awakening and deification for all whose spiritual natures were ripe for it.

A significant change which occurred in the hesychasm of the Russian layman was what one might call a more all-inclusive self-surrender to the power of the Sacred Name. In Near Eastern and Greek hesychasm there was still considerable emphasis on the control of one's mental processes and the acquisition of virtue through one's "own efforts." To many Russians it seemed as though complete self-surrender to the ineffable Divine Grace which issues forth from the Name of Jesus was lacking. A man cannot collect his mind or "constrain it to enter the heart" through "willing" it; all he can do is repeat the Sacred Name of Jesus, surrendering himself to it in all things and letting it carry him along. Thus Russian hesychasm as practiced by laymen and to a lesser degree as practiced by monks acquired a somewhat different flavor from that of Greece and the Near East. Not only was there a more complete abandonment to the power of the Sacred Name, but in Russia hesychasm merged with Russian kenotic mysticism as well as being influenced by the innate Russian veneration of nature and mother earth.

One must not, however, create a dichotomy between the hesychasm of Greece and the Near East and that of Russia. In the following essay, passages from both non-Russian and Russian writings will be utilized, although the primary emphasis will be on the Russian understanding of the significance of the Sacred Name of Jesus. For all hesychasts, the invocation of the Name has ultimately the same meaning and significance: it is a method of concentration or singlemindedness; it is a way of contemplation, recollection, and remembrance of God resulting in deification in Him; it is a way of worship and thanksgiving. Yet it is even more than this, for it is a way of life. Through the Sacred Name and in it man is initiated into the Divine mysteries. In the Name man dies and in it he comes to life, in it he sleeps and in it he awakens to the transfigured cosmos. Speaking of the invocation of the Sacred Name and of hesychasm in general, Patriarch Callistus writes:

> Although there are other ways and modes of life and, if you like, other practices . . . leading to salvation and giving peace to those who follow them, this one is preeminently the royal way, surpassing all other practices . . . since it renews the man completely and leads him to sonship of God, miraculously deifying in the Spirit him who follows it.[3]

THE INVOCATION OF THE SACRED NAME

IT IS related that there was once

> a monk of good life. One day a temptation beset him. He felt a great longing for some dried fish. And as it was impossible to get any in the monastery at that time, he was planning to go to the market and buy some. For a long while he struggled against the idea, and reasoned with himself that a monk ought to be content with the ordinary food provided for the brothers and by all means to avoid self-indulgence. Moreover, to walk about the market among crowds of people was also for a monk a source of temptation and unseemly. In the end . . . he, yielding to his self-will, made up his mind and went for the fish. After he left the building and was going

along the street, he noticed that his rosary was not in his hand, and he began to think: 'How comes this, that I am going like a soldier without his sword? This is most unseemly. And lay folk who meet me will . . . fall into temptation, seeing a monk without his rosary!' He was going back to get it, but, feeling in his pocket, he found it there. He pulled it out, crossed himself, and with his rosary in his hand went calmly on. As he got near the market he saw a horse standing by a shop with a great cartload of enormous tubs. All at once this horse, taking fright at something or other, bolted with all its might and with thundering hoofs made straight for him, grazing his shoulder and throwing him to the ground, though not hurting him very much. Then, a couple of paces from him, that load [of tubs] toppled over and the cart was smashed to splinters. Getting up quickly, naturally he was frightened enough, but at the same time he marveled how God had saved his life . . . Thinking no further about it, he bought the fish, went back, ate it, said his prayers, and lay down to sleep.[4]

That night a *starets* appeared to him in a dream, saying, "Do you see God's love for men?"

One might have expected the monk to understand the discovery that his rosary was missing as a sign of Divine disapproval of his plan, and his being thrown to the ground by the horse as a Divine judgment against his inexplicable and all-consuming desire for some dried fish, and that he would have immediately desisted from his plan and gone back to the monastery without the fish. This, however, was not the case. The whole incident did not disturb him in the least. Ostensibly this anecdote is introduced in *The Pilgrim Continues His Way* to exemplify the "power" of the Sacred Name of Jesus which the monk invoked with the aid of his rosary. So, too, it exemplifies the boundless Love of God which in the words of

Theophan the Hermit is "conceived . . . for us not through any necessity. . . . He loves us from Himself spontaneously, with love as much beyond measure as beyond understanding."[5]

Above all, the whole anecdote reveals quite concisely the basic "world outlook" of the devotee of the Sacred Name. The monk in question ceased struggling and reasoning with himself; he ceased acting as though he really had a "will" of his own. It is said in *The Pilgrim Continues His Way* that man

> hears the highest praise bestowed upon the beauty of virtue, he listens to censure of the baseness and misery of vice. . . . Guided in this way, one who ardently wishes for salvation sets off . . . But alas! even at the first step he finds it impossible to achieve his purpose. He foresees and even finds out by trial that his damaged and enfeebled nature will have the upper hand of the convictions of his mind, that his free will is bound, that his propensities are perverted, that his spiritual strength is but weakness.[6]

Man cannot acquire faith, true virtue, salvation or deification through his own efforts; he cannot "will" them. What then is left for him to do? He can continuously invoke the Sacred Name of Jesus; this he can do without either faith or virtue. This and this alone can man "will."

> God has assigned to the will and strength of man only the *quantity* of prayer. He has commanded unceasing prayer, always to pray [invoke the Sacred Name] at all times and in every place. By this secret method of achieving true prayer . . . faith, and the fulfilment of God's commandments, and salvation, are revealed. Thus, it is the quantity which is assigned to man as his share; frequency of prayer is his own, and within the province of his will. . . . What a sharp contrast with the moral

instructions of theoretical reason! . . . How simple and
easy a method! Yet it is tested by experience.[7]

Yet, properly speaking, unceasing prayer itself originates in
God and is said to be within the province of the devotee's
"will" only as a skillful means of making him realize that he
has no will. Only gradually is man able to relinquish all notions of himself as an independent "doer" and master of himself. In the words of Alexander d'Agapeyeff:

> A man deluding himself that he has 'will' (instead of
> a certain freedom of choice) and that he has everything
> under control, may decide to repeat the Jesus Prayer
> as a conscious invocation, say three thousand times. He
> starts, and before very long will, inevitably, find that
> his thoughts and emotions have taken control and that
> he is not in fact repeating the prayer. . . . If he is
> honest with himself he will see that he has no control
> over his thoughts or his emotions or even over his
> movements; that he has, in fact, no 'will,' and from this
> he will learn humility.[8]*

The devotee of the Sacred Name ceases to live a life of
pretense. Observing his inward state, plunging deeply into his
heart, he comes face to face with his own sinfulness. Being
honest with himself, he sees that he does not keep any of the
commandments, that he breaks them all—in thought if not in
deed—and that furthermore they are quite impossible to keep.
He ceases to hide under a cloak of self-righteousness; facade
upon facade falls; mask upon mask is cast aside until at last he
perceives his own nothingness and utter helplessness, thereby

* This perception does not in any way imply the Calvinist doctrine of
"predestination." Orthodox theology indeed asserts man's freedom or faculty
of inner determination. For a clarification of this whole problem see
Vladimir Lossky, *The Mystical Theology of the Eastern Church*, London,
1957, pp. 122, 125.

opening himself to the Divine Grace through which he awakens to deification in God and perceives His Presence in the entire realm of created being. Necessary to such awakening is the devotee's realization that even his externally virtuous actions very often have as their basis purely selfish, egocentric motives.

While profoundly aware of his egocentric depravity or fallen state and honestly admitting his total unrighteousness, the devotee of the Sacred Name knows no anxiety over his sinfulness. He does not despair, but gives up striving to become "better," striving to become something he is not. Realizing that he has no "will" of his own, he joyfully abandons himself to the all-powerful Divine Name which, if repeated unceasingly, "draws all things unto itself." Leaving all to the Name of Jesus, he lets it transform and awaken him. Indeed, at the core of hesychast teaching is the simple advice: *"Pray and think what you will," "pray and do what you will," "pray and do not labor much to conquer your passions by your own strength," "pray and fear nothing."*[9] Through unceasing prayer thoughts are purified, the passions of the mind and body are subdued and transformed, deeds become "selfless," and fear is banished.

> Pray somehow or other, only pray always and be disturbed by nothing. Be gay in spirit and peaceful. Prayer will arrange everything. . . . 'To pray somehow is within our power, but to pray purely is the gift of grace.' So offer to God what it is within your power to offer. . . .
>
> Now, do you see what profound thoughts are focused in that wise saying: 'Love, and do what you will'; 'pray, and do what you will'? How comforting and consoling is all this for the sinner overwhelmed by his weaknesses, groaning under the burden of his warring passions.[10]

By "prayer" is meant the Jesus Prayer alone. This is not a negation of other forms of prayer, the relevance of which, for those who are not devotees of the Sacred Name, is fully acknowledged. Isolated, individual prayer for specific things is, however, not practiced by most devotees of the Name, for it would defeat their very purpose of total self-surrender to the Divine Providence. For them, all other forms of non-liturgical prayer are quite superfluous as the Jesus Prayer is all-inclusive.

> We should throw all men into His Name and enclose
> them therein. Long lists of intercessions are not neces-
> sary. . . . All men . . . are already gathered together
> within the Name.[11]

The Sacred Name of Jesus possesses an efficacy of itself. It is far more than a symbol for there is in it all that Jesus is. "The Name is the symbol and bearer of the Person of Christ. . . . The presence of Jesus is the real content and substance of the Holy Name."[12] It may be noted that in the last century there has been a marked tendency, chiefly among the monks of Mount Athos, to make the Sacred Name an object of worship in the sense of *latria*. This is not surprising as for centuries the Name has been regarded as a mystery of mysteries due to its all-inclusiveness and its virtue of bringing about awakening and deification in God, not to mention its significance as the very Name and Word of God. Within the Name of Jesus the un-confinable God is confined, as it were; so too, within it is the entire mystery of the cosmos. It contains the myriad mysteries which one may perceive in whatever one sees, hears, feels, or smells. There is no single phenomenon of existence which is not a mystery—a grain of sand no less than the earth itself, the cry of a bird or the roar of the sea no less than the language of man. Every word or name uttered, every sound, is not only a mystery, but with the conjunction of certain circumstances is capable of causing a complete revolution of thought and experience.

If every sound, word, or name is not only a mystery, but is capable of producing most extraordinary effects when uttered, how much greater is the mystery and virtue of the Sacred Name, the Name of the Godman Who brings man redemption from the sinfulness of his egocentric state and reveals the way of awakening and liberation from the bonds of hell which hold him captive. No absolute dualism separates the Sacred Name from other sounds and names, yet its mystery and virtue are greater inasmuch as it is all-inclusive and is the very Name of God. Within it resides the overshadowing Mystery of the God-head; within it every particular name finds its innermost iden-tity. In a certain sense, there is not a single sound, word, or name uttered which is "outside" the Sacred Name. "All crea-tion mysteriously utters the Name of Jesus," writes a monk. "We shall say the Name of Jesus in union with all creation."[13] The mountains, the trees, the flowers, the wind, and the waves together with all sentient beings continually utter the Sacred Name and praise their Creator. In the words of a holy wan-derer, "The trees, the grass, the birds, the earth, the air, the light . . . all things prayed to God and sang His praise. Thus it was I came to understand what the *Philokalia* calls 'the knowl-edge of the speech of all creatures.' "[14]

The Sacred Name should be invoked without "self-effort" or calculation. The invocation should not be a contrived or deliberate act, but rather should proceed spontaneously from the depths of one's being—as natural and unlabored as the cry of a bird or the roar of the sea.

> The repetition of the Name may be likened to the beat-ing of wings by which a bird rises into the air. It must never be labored or forced or hurried . . . . It must be gentle, easy, and—let us give to this word its deepest meaning—graceful. . . . We must not come to the invo-

St. Simeon of Serbia—Serbian icon

cation of the Name through some whim or arbitrary decision of our own. We must be called to it, led to it by God.[15]

Yet, no limitations may be placed on the invocation of the Name. Ultimately even what appears to be a contrived invocation of "self-effort" is an invocation moved by the grace of God, and originates not in the devotee as an individual "I" but in God—"No man can say Lord Jesus but by the Holy Ghost" (I Cor. 12:3, Slavonic Version).

Continuous invocation of the Name, even when pronounced with neither faith nor devotion can produce most extraordinary effects through the infinite and mysterious virtue of the Sacred Name itself.

> The Name of Jesus invoked in prayer contains in itself self-existing and self-acting salutary power . . . therefore, do not be disturbed by the imperfection or dryness of your prayer . . . Do not listen to the inexperienced, thoughtless insinuation of the vain world that lukewarm invocation . . . is useless repetition. No; the power of the divine Name and frequent calling upon it will reveal its fruit in its season. . . . Do not silence the unbroken invocations of your prayer, although it may be that this cry of yours comes from a heart which is still at war with itself . . . Never mind! Only go on with it and don't let it be silenced and don't be disturbed. It will itself purify itself by repetition.[16]

However lacking in spontaneity in the beginning, the invocation of the Name starts a process of reintegration in the devotee, in whom both faith and humility are born as he suddenly finds himself invoking the Name effortlessly. Then he begins to become aware of the boundless Presence of Him Whose Name is the Sacred Name—first in himself and then in all creation, both animate and inanimate.

While invoking the Sacred Name, the devotee must be careful not to cultivate the "subjective" associations and images which the word or words of the invocation are liable to call forth.

> If . . . the mind is kept concentrated on the actual words of the prayer, or on some one definite idea of 'Jesus' which is bound up with them in the mind, then they may become an incantation, a formula which imprisons the mind instead of setting it free.[17]

Jesus must be accepted and invoked as He is, the whole Jesus of Sacred Tradition, Jesus the Godman—not only the Jesus of gentleness and love, but the Jesus Who cursed the fig tree and drove the money changers from the temple; not only the resurrected Jesus, but also the crucified Jesus Who cried, "My God, my God. Why hast Thou forsaken me?" The real Jesus, the whole Jesus must be invoked and not a sentimentalized, fragmented "Jesus" who is neither God nor man, much less God-man. If the devotee concentrates on his own individual notions of the Holy One Whose Name he is invoking or on those aspects of the Person of Jesus which appeal to him most, he only becomes more enslaved to the fantasies of prelest. Then he "becomes a dreamer instead of a hesychast," and may even fall victim to illusionary visions of Jesus, which in such a case are merely projections of the devotee's own psychic content—projections wherein the "demons of prelest" assume the form of angels of light and lead the devotee even deeper into the abyss of egocentricity while causing him to think that he is experiencing deification. It is to avoid such deceptions as this that the hesychasts regard the guidance of an experienced *starets* as quite indispensable for all who practice "unceasing prayer."

As visions are discouraged—although the possibility of true visions is acknowledged—so too is any interest in or preoccupation with the "psychic" or "occult," for these have no bearing on awakening. "Beware of taking your visions† for direct revelations of grace," writes a holy wanderer. "For these things may often happen quite naturally in the order of things."[18] Indeed, many people quite lacking in holiness and very far from awakening possess various psychic powers and frequently engage in "occult exhibitionism" which only leads them deeper into egocentricity and illusion. Nothing is more dangerous, indeed nothing has greater diabolical possibilities than psychic power divorced from holiness; it is only in the hands of a true saint that such power is not dangerous. The holy man may possess a high degree of psychic sensitivity; he may be clairvoyant, have foreknowledge, and be able to levitate. Yet, he never indulges himself in the psychic for the divertissement of the curious, but utilizes it only in a timely and well-controlled manner, as, for example, in discerning the hidden illusions which cloud the minds of those in his spiritual care in order to advise and lead them to the sanctified state. If the devotee of the Sacred Name suddenly finds his psychic sensitivity increased, he pays no attention to it and in no way deludes himself into thinking that it is a sign of sanctity.

Unceasing repetition of the Sacred Name "collects the mind from its customary circling and wandering." "Again and again the mind must be brought back to the prayer until one realizes that the mind is indeed like 'a wagon load of monkeys,' "[19] states Alexander d'Agapeyeff. Gradually the mind ceases to cling to the thoughts and images which arise in it; gradually it becomes freed "from the ever-turbulent and ever-present stream of thoughts, words, impressions, pictures, and day dreams, which keep one asleep."[20] Thus realizing purity of mind, the devotee becomes receptive to the all-consuming flame of the Deity within the depths of his heart and begins to awaken to his true self which hitherto had been concealed by his state of inner dispersion. Indeed, all which had previously seemed to be "his self" is seen to be but illusion, mere masks

† Here "visions" refers specifically to "clairvoyant" insight.

and façades through which he evaded his true self and the
Indwelling Godhead. "The trouble is that we live far from
ourselves and have but little wish to get any nearer to ourselves," states a holy wanderer. "Indeed we are running away
all the time to avoid coming face to face with our real selves."[21]
Through the ineffable grace which issues forth from unceasing
invocation of the Divine Name man "returns to himself"; he is
made whole and is liberated from all anxiety, conflict, and
indecision. "By the power of the name of Jesus," writes Bishop
Ignati, "the mind is freed from doubt, indecision and hesitation."[22] In the words of a monk:

> No prayer is simpler than this 'one-word prayer' in
> which the Holy Name becomes the only focus of the
> whole life. Complicated methods often tire. . . . But
> the Name of Jesus easily gathers everything into itself.
> It has a power of unification and integration. The di-
> vided personality which could say: 'My name is legion,
> for we are many' will recover its wholeness in the sacred
> Name.[23]

The devotee of the Name who has realized purity of mind
becomes, in a certain sense, like a small child—"Truly I tell
you, unless you turn and become like children, you will never
enter the kingdom of heaven."* As a small child trusts in his
parents and knows no anxiety, the devotee of the Name trusts
in the Fatherly Providence; like a small child he lives in the
present, is unconcerned with the past or future, and acts spontaneously, without thought; like a small child he perceives all
things as infinitely miraculous and mysterious. There is a cer-

---

* This is not to say that children are awakened, sanctified beings free
from all illusion and egocentricity. Indeed, most children become su-
premely egocentric at a very early age. Nevertheless the child possesses
certain characteristics in common with the holy man as well as with the
devotee of the Name who has not realized full awakening.

tain innocence and simplicity in a child which is not unlike that of the saint. Bishop Ignati writes:

> The most sublime mental activity is extraordinarily simple. It needs for its acceptance childlike simplicity. . . . But we have become so complicated that it is just this simplicity which is inaccessible, incomprehensible to us. We want to be clever. . . . It is for this reason that we need a guide [the Church, the Name, and a *starets*] to lead us out of our complexity, out of our cuteness, out of our cunning, out of our vanity.[24]

The devotee of the Name should not be in any way preoccupied about the future—"Let us not regard our prayer in relation to fulfillment in the future, but in relation to fulfillment *in Jesus now*."[25] Not only does the devotee have no care for himself in regard to his physical needs, but also does not concern himself with eschatological matters or the future life. Bishop Ignati says, "Let us practice the prayer of Jesus disinterestedly, with simplicity and purity of intention . . . with complete surrender to the will of God, with hope and trust in the wisdom, goodness, and omnipotence of His holy will."[26] When the invocation of the Sacred Name is practiced chiefly out of concern for the future life, purity of intention is lacking. Yet for some beings thought of "future rewards and punishments" is quite necessary in order to arouse them from the "sleep of death." St. Tikhon Zadonsky once said that "God sometimes attracts us by promises of rewards, 'as one can attract a small child with an apple.' "[27] Likewise, it is written in *The Pilgrim Continues His Way* that

> in their experience and godly wisdom, the holy Fathers, knowing the weakness . . . of man, take a special line about it, and in this respect put jam with the powder and smear the edge of the medicine cup with honey.[28]

It is thus that some advise thinking of the rewards of unceasing invocation of the Name as an enticement for the weak, that they might be "enticed to put the practice of prayer to test." Many are the enticements and skillful means utilized by God in order to bring about awakening, and chief among them is the very root of man's sinfulness and sleep of death—his self-love, his continual preoccupation with himself.

> The root, the head, and the strength of all passions and actions in man is his innate love of self. . . . Innate self-love, the principal element in life, is a deep-seated stimulus to prayer in the natural man. The all-wise Creator of all things has imbued the nature of a man with a capacity for self-love precisely as an 'enticement,' to use the expression of the Fathers, which will draw the fallen being of man upward.[29]

Whereas thought of rewards and punishments in the future life may function as an enticement for the weak, thought of the past events of one's life and anxiety over one's past sins serve no salutary purpose whatsoever. To be sure, man should acknowledge his sinfulness, but he should not brood over or be preoccupied with his past sins. Above all, he should not allow them to oppress him. Theophan the Hermit says, "You will always recognize, as coming from the devil, every recollection of sins, which has the power to oppress and cast you into despair."[30] Likewise he writes:

> It is wrong to regard as a virtue the excessive grief, which men feel after committing a sin, not realizing that it is caused by pride and a high opinion of themselves. . . . For by thinking that they are something important they undertake too much, hoping to deal with it themselves. When the experience of their downfall shows them how weak they are, they are astounded. . . . They are cast into turmoil and grow fainthearted.

For they see, fallen and prone on the ground, that graven image which is themselves . . . This does not happen to a humble man who trusts in God.[31]

St. Isaac of Syria asks, "What is repentance?" and answers "Abandoning what has been."[32]

It is related that once there were two Egyptian hermits who, after leading rigidly ascetic lives in desert caves for many years, were suddenly tempted by the devil. Taking the reed baskets they had made, they set off to Alexandria where they sold the baskets and spent three days and nights in debauchery. Having spent all their money by the fourth day, they started back to their desert cells.

One of them wept bitterly and howled aloud. The other walked at his side . . . and sang psalms joyfully to himself. The first cried:

'Accursed that I am, now am I lost forever . . . All my fasts and hymns and prayers have been in vain. I might as well have sinned all the time; all lost in one foul moment! Alas! Alas!'

But the other hermit went on singing, quietly, joyfully.

'What!' cried the first hermit. 'Have you gone out of your mind?'

'Why?' asked the joyful one.

'Why don't you repent?'

'What is there for me to repent of?' asked the joyful one.

'And Alexandria, have you forgotten it?' asked his companion.

'What of Alexandria? Glory be to the Almighty Who preserves that famous and honorable town!'

'But what did we do in Alexandria?'

'What did we do? Why, we sold our baskets, prayed before the ikon of Holy St. Mark, visited several churches, walked a little in the town . . . , conversed with the virtuous and Christly Leonila. . . .'

The [falsely] repentant hermit stared at the other in pale stupefaction.

'And the house of ill-fame in which we spent the night . . .' said he.

'God preserve us!' said the other. 'The evening and night we spent in the guesthouse of the patriarch.'

'Holy martyrs! God has already blasted his reason,' cried the [falsely] repentant hermit. 'And with whom did you get drunk on Tuesday night? Tell me that.'

'We partook of wine and viands in the refectory of the patriarchate, Tuesday being the festival of the Presentation of the most Blessed Mother of God.'

'Poor fellow! And whom did we kiss?'

'We were honored at parting with a holy kiss from that father of fathers, the most blessed Archbishop of the great city of Alexandria . . .'

'Ah, why do you make a mock of me? Does it mean that after yesterday's abominations the devil has entered into possession of you . . .'

'I can't say in whom the devil has found a home, in me or in you,' said the other, 'in me when I rejoice in God's gifts and His holy will, when I praise the Creator and all His works, or in you who rave and call the house of our most blessed father and pastor a house of ill-fame . . .'

'Ah, you heretic!' screamed the [falsely] repentant hermit. 'Arian monster!'

They arrived back at their caves, and one beat his head on the rock all night and tore his hair and made the desert echo with his howls and shrieks, while the other calmly and joyfully went on singing psalms. In the morning the former brooded

and brooded over his sins in Alexandria, finally deciding that
he was irrecoverably lost. Therefore he left his cave forever
and returned to Alexandria where he led a life of dissipation
for many years, finally being condemned to death after having
killed and robbed a wealthy merchant. In the meantime his old
companion continued to lead a holy life in his cave. Always
joyful, his sanctity was very great and he became renowned as a
starets and thaumaturge. At his death the odor of heavenly
incense filled the air, and it was not long before a great monastery was built over his holy relics.[33]

> The lesson of this story is, according to Varsonophy,
> who told it, that there are no sins of any importance
> except despondency. Did not both these hermits sin
> alike and yet but one of them was lost, namely, he
> who desponded?
>
> Varsonophy was a pilgrim from Mount Athos, who
> used to say, '. . . don't grieve about your sins, be done
> with them, they don't count. . . . If to sin is evil, then
> to remember sin is evil. . . . There is only one deadly
> sin and that is despondency, from despondency comes
> despair, that is more than sin, that is spiritual death.'[34]

The above anecdote illustrates quite well, although in a
rather hyperbolic fashion and without stressing the necessity of
first acknowledging one's sinfulness, the meaning of true repentance which is "abandoning what has been." "Compared
with God's providence and God's mercy the trespasses of all
flesh are as a handful of sand thrown into the sea,"[35] writes
St. Isaac of Syria. The sinfulness of man, the egocentricity of
his every thought and deed, cannot be denied. Yet his "will" is
tied on every side and his very sins "do not happen without
God's leave."

His salvation consists in acknowledging his sinfulness
with humility, while at the same time acknowledging the in-

dwelling Christ, the Holy One Who sacrifices and gives Himself to man, taking the sins of the world upon Himself and freeing man from "the great curse of prelest."

Patriarch Callistus says that there is no unforgivable sin, and Theophan the Hermit writes, "Never admit a shadow of doubt about forgiveness. Forgiveness is already fully prepared and the record of all sins has been torn up on the Cross."[36] God forgives man his sins, which He has taken upon Himself, but man must forgive himself as well as be forgiven by God—not by denying that he is sinful, but by abandoning his sins to God. Through unceasing invocation of the Sacred Name —not in any way negating the necessity of sacramental confession—man is reconciled with God and with himself. "Abandoning what has been," he realizes the forgiveness of God and he forgives himself.

> St. John Karpathisky in *The Philokalia* says that when in the Prayer of Jesus we call upon the Holy Name and say, 'Have mercy on me, a sinner,' then to every such petition the Voice of God answers in secret, 'Son, thy sins be forgiven.'[37]

In the words of a monk:

> The Name of Jesus brings forgiveness and reconciliation. . . . After sin let us not 'hang about,' delay and linger. Let us not hesitate to take up again the invocation of the Name, in spite of our unworthiness. A new day is breaking and Jesus stands on the shore. . . . He comes to us at that moment and as we are. He begins again where He has left us, or rather, where we have left Him. . . . He does not require from us long apologies for the past, but He wants us to mix, as before, His Person and His Name with the detail and routine of our life—with our broiled fish and our honeycomb.[38]

In its final stage the invocation of the Sacred Name becomes "the silent prayer of the heart." "The direct link is created between body and spirit. . . . Now the prayer enters the heart and lives Itself with every heartbeat."[39] Thus the devotee "stands in the presence of God without any means or intermediary."[40] Returning to the "primitive contemplative state in which he issued from the hands of his Creator,"[41] he awakens to deification in Him Whose Name he has been invoking and begins "to live, breathe, sleep and wake, walk, eat and drink with Him and in Him."[42]

> The sleep of negligence and ignorance ceases; then the drowsiness of sloth and despondency is whisked from the eyelids . . . then conflicts, pollutions, and movements cease.[43]

Having realized a state of selfless purity, by virtue of this very fact, the holy man cannot but accept into his being the impurity of all who are impure, at the same time giving to them "his own" purity which is "their" purity through the interpenetration of all things—just as Jesus, the Supreme Holy One and Godman, took the sins of the world upon Himself. Thus the greatest of saints always claim to be the worst of sinners; thus the barrier which superficially seems to separate the saint from sinner, the pure from the impure, vanishes. The devotee of the Name who has realized deification in God makes no distinctions. The differentiations which seem to separate one man from another are seen to be but superficial, for the Sacred Name of Jesus embraces all beings within itself. He perceives Jesus in every man and does not distinguish between the most or the least sinful, king or beggar, Christian or non-Christian. St. Mark the Ascetic writes:

> The soul which is inwardly united to God becomes, in the greatness of its joy, like a good-natured simple-

hearted child, and now condemns no one, Greek, heathen, Jew nor sinner, but looks at them all alike with sight that has been cleansed, [and] finds joy in the whole world.[44]

Through continually invoking the Name of Jesus, the devotee awakens to the non-dual Theocentric cosmos wherein the Uncreated Light overshadows and encloses "all in all" within itself. Abandoning himself to God, he awakens to the Presence of God within himself and all creation, in which "the Lamb slain from the foundation of the world" continues to sacrifice and give Himself. To conclude with the words of an anonymous monk:

The Name of Jesus helps us to transfigure the world into Christ (without any pantheistic confusion). . . . What we call the inanimate world is carried along by a Christward movement. . . . It is the utterance of this Name that Christians should hear in nature. By pronouncing the Name of Jesus upon the natural things, upon a stone or a tree, a fruit or a flower, the sea or a landscape, or whatever it is, the believer speaks aloud the secret of these things. . . .

The animal world may also be transfigured by us. . . . If we invoke the Name of Jesus upon the animals, we give them back their primitive dignity which we so easily forget—the dignity of living beings . . . in Jesus . . .

It is mainly in relation to men that we can exercise

Christ Triumphant—Fresco at the Dechani Monastery, Serbia

a ministry of transfiguration. The risen Christ appeared several times under an aspect which was no
longer the one his disciples knew . . . It was each time
in the form of an ordinary man such as we may meet
in our everyday life. Jesus thus illustrated an important aspect of his presence among us—his presence in
man. He was thus completing what he had taught:
'I was an hungered, and ye gave me meat. I was thirsty
and ye gave me drink . . . naked and ye clothed me. I
was sick, and ye visited me. I was in prison, and ye
came unto me . . . Inasmuch as ye have done it unto
one of the least of these my brethren, ye have done it
unto me.' . . . Everybody can . . . at any time and in any
place, see the Face of Our Lord. Men of today are
realistically minded . . . and, when the saints and the
mystics come and tell them: 'We have seen the Lord,'
they answer with Thomas: 'Except I shall . . . thrust my
hand into his side, I will not believe.' Jesus accepts this
challenge. He allows Himself to be seen, and touched,
and spoken to. . . . Jesus shows us the poor, and the sick,
and the sinners, and generally all men, and tells us:
'Behold my hands and my feet . . . Handle me and see;
for a spirit hath not flesh and bones, as ye see me
have.' Men and women are the flesh and bones, the
hands and feet, the pierced side of Christ—His mystical
Body. In them we can experience the reality of the
Resurrection and the real presence (though without confusion of essence) of the Lord Jesus. . . . The Name of
Jesus is a concrete and powerful means of transfiguring
men into their hidden, innermost, utmost reality. We
should approach all men . . . with the Name of Jesus
in our heart and on our lips. We should pronounce
His Name over them all, for their real name is the
Name of Jesus. Name them with His Name, within

His Name. . . . Adore Christ in them, serve Christ in them. In many of these men and women—in the malicious, in the criminal—Jesus is imprisoned. Deliver Him by silently recognizing and worshipping Him in them. If we go through the world with this new vision, saying 'Jesus' over every man, seeing Jesus in every man, everybody will be transformed and transfigured.[45]

REFERENCES

I. Eastern Orthodoxy—An Introduction

1 Nicholas Zernov, *The Church of the Eastern Christians*, p. 39.
2 *Ibid.*, pp. 53-54.
3 Fr. Sergius Bulgakov, *The Orthodox Church*, p. 68.
4 George Fedotov, *The Russian Religious Mind*, p. 33.
5 Leonid Ouspensky and Vladimir Lossky, *The Meaning of Icons*, p. 41.
6 Fedotov, *op. cit.*, p. 55.
7 Zernov, *op. cit.*, p. 35.
8 Alexei Hackel, *The Icon*, p. 14.
9 Pierre Van Paassen, *Visions Rise and Change*, p. 251.

II. Some Aspects of the Russian Religious Consciousness

1 N. B. Gogol, *Meditations on the Divine Liturgy* (London, 1913), p. 2.
2 Fedotov, *op. cit.*, p. 102.
3 Quoted in Van Paassen, *op. cit.*, p. 154.
4 Iulia de Beausobre, *Creative Suffering*, p. 35.
5 Nadejda Gorodetzky, *The Humiliated Christ in Modern Russian Thought*, p. 180.
6 de Beausobre, *op. cit.*, p. 34.
7 *Ibid.*, p. 37.
8 Quoted in Van Paassen, *op. cit.*, p. 71.
9 George Fedotov (compiler), *A Treasury of Russian Spirituality* (London, 1951), p. 335. (Italics the author's.)

10 ———, *The Russian Religious Mind,* p. 12.
11 *The Way of a Pilgrim* (R. M. French, trans.), p. 106.
12 Feodor Dostoyevsky, *The Brothers Karamazov* (Constance Garnett, trans.), New York, 1943, pp. 382-385.

III. TEACHINGS OF THE HESYCHASTS

1 Fr. Basil Krivosheine, *The Ascetic and Theological Teachings of (Saint) Gregory Palamas,* p. 5.
2 *Philokalia I,** p. 268.
3 *Philokalia II,* p. 272.
4 Krivosheine, *op. cit.,* p. 18.
5 *Ibid.,* p. 24.
6 *Ibid.,* p. 17.
7 Quoted in Frithjof Schuon, *The Transcendent Unity of Religions,* p. 177.
8 Bishop Ignati Brianchininov, *On the Prayer of Jesus,* p. 69.
9 *Philokalia II,* p. 22.
10 *Loc. cit.*
11 *Unseen Warfare,†* p. 243.
12 *Ibid.,* p. 221.
13 *Ibid.,* p. 72.
14 *Ibid.,* p. 82.
15 *Philokalia I,* p. 330.
16 *Philokalia II,* p. 260.
17 *Ibid.,* p. 23.
18 *Ibid.,* p. 30.

* PHILOKALIA I *designates* EARLY FATHERS FROM THE PHILOKALIA.

PHILOKALIA II *designates* WRITINGS FROM THE PHILOKALIA ON THE PRAYER OF THE HEART.

† *It should be noted that as* UNSEEN WARFARE *stands as revised and edited by Theophan the Hermit, all quotations from it have been credited to him.*

19 Krivosheine, *op. cit.*, p. 6.
20 *Unseen Warfare*, p. 66.
21 *Philokalia II*, p. 309.
22 *Philokalia I*, p. 177.
23 *Ibid.*, p. 196. (Italics the author's.)
24 *Philokalia II*, p. 235. (Slight grammatical changes by author.)
25 *Ibid.*, p. 37.
26 *Ibid.*, p. 289.
27 *Ibid.*, p. 305.
28 *Ibid.*, p. 308.
29 *Ibid.*, p. 193.
30 *Ibid.*, p. 235.
31 *Ibid.*, p. 386.
32 *Ibid.*, p. 311.
33 *Philokalia I*, p. 210.
34 *Ibid.*, p. 357.
35 Brianchininov, *op. cit.*, p. 46.
36 *Unseen Warfare*, p. 217.
37 Krivosheine, *op. cit.*, p. 44.
38 *Philokalia II*, p. 141.
39 Krivosheine, *op. cit.*, p. 41.
40 *Ibid.*, p. 18.
41 *Ibid.*, p. 20.
42 *Ibid.*, p. 23.
43 *Loc. cit.*
44 Krivosheine, *op. cit.*, p. 43.
45 *Ibid.*, p. 40.
46 *Philokalia I*, p. 226.
47 H. A. Hodges, in "Introduction" to *Unseen Warfare*, pp. 23-24.
48 *Ibid.*, p. 24.
49 See Iulia de Beausobre, *Flame in the Snow*, p. 147, Stephan Graham, *The Way of Mary and the Way of Martha*, p. 128, and George Fedotov, *A Treasury of Russian Spirituality*, p. 273 for varying accounts of this incident.
50 Krivosheine, *op. cit.*, p. 34.

51 Bishop Innocent, *Indication of the Way into the Kingdom of Heaven* (New York, 1952), p. 29.
52 *Philokalia I*, p. 225 (Italics the author's.)
53 *Ibid.*, pp. 29, 33.
54 *The Pilgrim Continues His Way*, p. 185.
55 *Philokalia I*, p. 212.
56 *Ibid.*, p. 189.
57 Vladimir Soloviev, *La justification du bien* (Paris, 1939), p. 72.
58 *Unseen Warfare*, p. 201.
59 *Ibid.*, p. 187.
60 *Philokalia I*, p. 192.
61 *Unseen Warfare*, pp. 265, 269.
62 *Philokalia I*, p. 242.
63 *Ibid.*, p. 347.

IV. THE INVOCATION OF THE SACRED NAME

1 Brianchininov, *op. cit.*, p. 17.
2 *Ibid.*, p. 48.
3 *Philokalia II*, p. 268.
4 *The Pilgrim Continues His Way*, pp. 135-137.
5 *Unseen Warfare*, p. 230.
6 *The Pilgrim Continues His Way*, p. 184.
7 *Ibid.*, p. 190.
8 Alexander d'Agapeyeff, "Introduction" to *On the Prayer of Jesus*, p. viii.
9 See *The Pilgrim Continues His Way*, p. 207.
10 *Ibid.*, pp. 208-209.
11 Anonymous Monk, *On the Invocation of the Name of Jesus*, p. 20.
12 *Ibid.*, p. 12.
13 *Ibid.*, p. 17.
14 *The Way of a Pilgrim*, p. 31.

15 Anon. Monk, *op. cit.*, pp. 6, 8.
16 *The Pilgrim Continues His Way*, p. 194.
17 Hodges, *op. cit.*, p. 26.
18 *The Way of a Pilgrim*, p. 104.
19 d'Agapeyeff, *op. cit.*, p. v.
20 *Ibid.*, p. ix.
21 *The Way of a Pilgrim*, p. 89.
22 Brianchininov, *op. cit.*, p. 11.
23 Anon. Monk, *op. cit.*, p. 9.
24 Brianchininov, *op. cit.*, p. 29.
25 Anon. Monk, *op. cit.*, p. 13.
26 Brianchininov, *op. cit.*, p. 104.
27 Nadejda Gorodetzky, *St. Tikhon Zadonsky* (London, 1951), p. 101.
28 *The Pilgrim Continues His Way*, p. 211.
29 *Ibid.*, pp. 215-216.
30 *Unseen Warfare*, p. 254.
31 *Ibid.*, p. 88.
32 *Philokalia II*, p. 219.
33 Stephan Graham, *op. cit.*, pp. 157-161 (slight grammatical changes made by author).
34 *Ibid.*, p. 161.
35 *Philokalia I*, p. 275.
36 *Unseen Warfare*, p. 158.
37 *The Pilgrim Continues His Way*, p. 137.
38 Anon. Monk, *op. cit.*, p. 14.
39 d'Agapeyeff, *op. cit.*, p. vi.
40 Brianchininov, *op. cit.*, p. 13.
41 *The Pilgrim Continues His Way*, p. 226.
42 *Philokalia II*, p. 173.
43 Brianchininov, *op. cit.*, p. 41.
44 *The Pilgrim Continues His Way*, p. 160.
45 Anon. Monk, *op. cit.*, pp. 17-20.

SELECTED BIBLIOGRAPHY

ANONYMOUS MONK, *On the Invocation of the Name of Jesus.* London: The Fellowship of St. Alban and St. Sergius, 1953.

——, *Orthodox Spirituality.* London: The Fellowship of St. Alban and St. Sergius, 1946.

ARSENIEV, NICHOLAS, *Holy Moscow.* London: S.P.C.K., 1940.

> (An interesting account of Russian religious life during the last century.)

——, *Mysticism and the Eastern Church.* London: S.C.M., 1926.

ATTWATER, DONALD, *The Christian Churches of the East,* Vol. II. Milwaukee: Bruce, 1947. (pp. 6-183.)

> (This book contains many interesting facts regarding Orthodoxy which are not readily available elsewhere in English. The reader should be advised, however, that the author of this work is a Western Catholic and therefore makes occasional statements which are unacceptable from the Orthodox point of view.)

DE BEAUSOBRE, IULIA, *Creative Suffering.* Westminster: Dacre Press, 1940.

——, *Flame in the Snow.* London: Constable, 1946.

> (Deals with the life of St. Seraphim of Sarov.)

BRIANCHININOV, BISHOP IGNATI, *On the Prayer of Jesus.* Trans. by Fr. Lazarus, with an Introduction by Alexander d'Agapeyeff. London: John Watkins, 1952.

BULGAKOV, FR. SERGIUS, *The Orthodox Church.* London: Centenary Press, 1935.

DAWKINS, R. M., *The Monks of Athos*. London: Allen and Unwin, 1936.

FEDOTOV, GEORGE, *The Russian Religious Mind*. Cambridge: Harvard University Press, 1946.

FRENCH, R. M., trans., *The Way of a Pilgrim* and *The Pilgrim Continues His Way*. London: S.P.C.K., 1954.
> (Published by Harper & Brothers in U.S.)

GORODETZKY, NADEJDA, *The Humiliated Christ in Modern Russian Thought*. London: S.P.C.K., 1938.

GRAHAM, STEPHAN, *The Way of Martha and the Way of Mary*. New York: Macmillan, 1917.

———, *With the Russian Pilgrims to Jerusalem*. London: Macmillan, 1914.
> (Although these two books contain some quite erroneous notions of Orthodox spirituality, they nevertheless reveal many profound insights and give excellent accounts of religious life in old Russia.)

HACKEL, ALEXEI, *The Icon*. Freiburg im Breisgau: Herder and Co. GmbH., 1954.

KADLOUBOVSKY, E. AND PALMER, G. E. H., trans., *Early Fathers from the Philokalia*. London: Faber and Faber, 1954.

———, *Unseen Warfare*. With an Introduction by H. A. Hodges. London: Faber and Faber, 1951.

———, *Writings from the Philokalia on the Prayer of the Heart*. London: Faber and Faber, 1951.

KRIVOSHEINE, FR. BASIL, *The Ascetic and Theological Teachings of (St.) Gregory Palamas*. Eastern Churches Quarterly Reprint, 1954.

LOT-BORODINE, MME., "La doctrine de la deification dans l'eglise grecque," in *Revue de l'Histoire des Religions,* t. CV and CVI (1932).

OUSPENSKY, LEONID AND LOSSKY, VLADIMIR, *The Meaning of Icons.* Boston: Boston Book and Art Shop, 1952.

SCHUBART, WALTER, *Russia and Western Man.* New York: Ungar, 1950.

> (A profound and stimulating study of the Russian spirit presented in contrast to that of Western Europe, by a convert to Eastern Orthodoxy.)

SCHUON, FRITHJOF, *The Transcendent Unity of Religions.* New York: Pantheon, 1953.

> (See ch. IX-2, p. 176 for a discussion of hesychasm.)

VAN PAASSEN, PIERRE, *Visions Rise and Change.* New York: Dial Press, 1955 c.

> (An objective account of the religious situation in Soviet Russia.)

ZERNOV, NICOLAS, *The Church of the Eastern Christians.* London: S.P.C.K., 1947.

———, *Moscow, Third Rome.* London: S.P.C.K., 1937.

INDEX

The letter n following a page number indicates footnote

www.ingramcontent.com/pod-product-compliance
Lightning Source LLC
Chambersburg PA
CBHW021507090426
42739CB00007B/500